Money Manipulation

and

Social Order

By Rev. Denis Fahey, C.S.SP., D.D., D.PH., B.A.

Professor of Philosophy and Church History, Holy Ghost Missionary College,
Kimmage, Dublin

"No servant can serve two masters . . .. you cannot serve God and mammon. Now the Pharisees, who were covetous, heard all these things: and they derided Him."

Saint Luke 16:13-14

Imprimi Potest: D. Murphy, C. S. Sp.,

Praep. Prov. Hib.

Nihil Obstat: P. Sexton, D.D.,

Censor Deputatus.

Imprimatur: Daniel,

†*Episcopus Corcagiensis*
Corcagiae 11a *Maii*, 1944

First Printing 1944
First Loreto Printing October, 2010
ISBN: 1-930278-97-7
Printed in the United States of America

Loreto Publications
P. O. Box 603 Fitzwilliam, NH 03447
www.loretopubs.org • Tele: 603.239.6671

Dedication

To the Immaculate Queen of Heaven and Earth, to Saint Joseph, the Head of the Holy Family and the Protector of the Universal Church, to Saint Thomas Aquinas, the Catholic Church's official teacher of order, and to Saint Brigid of Ireland, who was so well-versed in the arts of rural life, this book is lovingly and humbly dedicated by the author, in the hope that by their intercession it may contribute in some little way to the return of the world to the full acceptance of the rule of Christ the King, so that social environment may once more sustain men in their efforts to live as members of his Mystical Body.

"I have alluded to the appalling progress of desert-making on behalf of greed throughout the world. Erosion is a symptom of sickness in any civilization. Today, as modern civilization is a world complex, it bids fair to engulf mankind. Already the specter of world famine casts its shadow ahead. Even in forestry there is more need to plant trees to preserve life than there is to exploit forests for felling. The financial rulers have the greatest responsibility for all this, since the system they administer has faithfully implemented human greed and ignorance. Financial greed has not only led the van, but directed the attack; and, having lent at interest sufficient money to exploit the soil, it has thereafter diverted the springs of credit that might have repaired the damage due to soil exploitation to the profitable business of transport, public utilities and luxury trades. The result is that it is as devastating to human material as it has been upon the soil . . .. Most of this degeneration can be laid finally at the door of finance, just as to the same door we can lay the twenty to thirty million unemployed who haunted the streets of Europe and America." (*Alternative to Death,* by the Earl of Portsmouth, pp. 40, 37).

Table of Contents

Loreto's Introduction to Father Denis Fahey

When Jesus Christ, our King and Master, taught us how to pray to His Father and Our Father, he used the phrase "thy kingdom come, thy will be done, on *earth* as it is in heaven." In heaven God's will is perfectly accomplished, but here on earth, fallen mankind cannot fulfill God's will without the constant assistance of sanctifying grace communicated to the world through the sacraments of His church.

After the fall of Adam, a world perfectly ordered to God's divine will was corrupted and **dis**-order became the 'natural' state of mankind and the created universe. It was the role of the Messias to **re**-order this fallen world—to bring a new state of order to the world His Father had created. The means for establishing that order by which a fallen world may return to God is the Catholic church and the life of sanctifying grace. As Christians newly born into the life of grace—a 'supernatural' state of being—we are all called to bring as much order to this world as is possible, all the while never forgetting that this world is in a fallen and corrupted state and that a 'utopia' is not possible here on earth. The Church of Christ is constantly opposed in this mission by all of the forces of 'naturalism' or **dis**-order, that is those forces opposed to the supernatural life of divine grace. It is the duty of all Christians of the Church Militant to battle against these forces.

This calling of Christians to the battle for order was the motto of the pontificate of Pope Saint X. That motto was *Instaurare Omnia in Christo,* "to restore all things in Christ", taken from Saint Paul's letter to the Ephesians 1:10. The modern popes have frequently warned us of the dangers of 'naturalism', which denies the supernatural life of grace and militates against it, and they have called us to fight in our private and public lives against this pernicious error. No priest has heeded that call and risen to defend the supernatural life of grace as clearly and as vigorously as Father Denis Fahey. He truly understood, and explained why, there is no salvation outside the Catholic church, either for individual persons or for the life of <u>society</u> and of <u>nations</u>.

A clear image of just what the life of a Christian *in a society imbued from top to bottom with the social principles of Christ the King* would be like, is not a widely shared understanding in much of the Christian world today, especially in America. We must remember that Christianity is a religion of world conquest! We are called to conquer the world for Christ and to do all that we can to subdue persons and nations to His will. A Catholic undertakes this battle first within himself and then within his family. Soon the influence of many families begins to pervade the community and then the nation or state. If Christian people do not have the full picture in their mind of exactly what God's Plan for Order in this world would look like in its accomplishment, then they can have no long-term strategy for victory and little hope of achieving it. We have all of the tools required and all of the powers of heaven backing us. Let us take into our hearts and our minds the full plan and its potential for the realization of peace in the world and Christ the King of heaven and earth will bless our efforts. This was the permanent admonition of Fr. Fahey.

Father Fahey was a seminarian and was ordained in Rome during the pontificate of Pius X. The young priest was deeply influenced and inspired by that pope. When he penned a short *Apologia* for his work, Father Fahey expressed his vocation in this fashion:

> "When in Rome I began to realize more fully the real significance of the history of the world, as the account of the acceptance and rejection of Our Lord's Program for Order. I used to ask permission to remain at the Confession of St. Peter, while the other scholastics went round the basilica.
>
> "I spent the time there going over the history of the world, and I repeatedly promised Saint Peter that if I ever got the chance, I would teach the truth about his Master in the way he and his successors, the Roman Pontiffs, wanted it done.
>
> That is what I have striven to do and am doing."

Father Fahey not only clarified, explained, taught, and defended 'Our Lord's Program for Order' in the world, he also actively fought and exposed the persons who were the enemies of that order. Because he did so, he has often been called 'negative' or 'anti-Semitic', or 'much too concerned with Masonic conspiracies'. These are the pathetic terms of opprobrium hurled with such energy by those enemies of Christ whose plans he has effectively opposed. But in this he was in good company with St. Louis Marie de Montfort and Our Lady, who appears 'terrible as an army set in battle array' to the enemies of her divine son.

Listen to the words of St. Louis Marie as he stresses the two functions of our Blessed Mother, the *positive* one of making Our Lord known, and the *negative* one of making war upon His enemies.

> Mary must be manifested more than ever by her mercy, her power and her grace in these latter times; by her mercy, bringing back and lovingly welcoming the poor strayed sinners who will be converted and will return to the Catholic Church; by her power, against the enemies of God, idolaters, schismatics, Mohammedans, Jews, and men hardened in impiety, who will rise in terrible revolt to seduce all those who oppose them and to make them fall by promises and threats; she must also be made manifest by her grace animating and sustaining the valiant soldiers and faithful servants of Jesus Christ, who shall battle for His interests.
>
> And lastly, Mary must be terrible to the devil and his ministers, as an army in battle array, principally in these latter times, because the devil knowing that he has but little time, and now less than ever, to damn souls, will every day redouble his efforts and his combats. He will before long raise up cruel persecutions and will lay terrible snares for the faithful servants and true children of Mary whom he finds more difficult to conquer than the others.

Loreto Publications is committed to re-issuing all of the previously published works of Fr. Fahey and making them available to a much wider audience. The works of Fr. Fahey are critically important for Catholics to read, understand, and disseminate in our day when the forces of 'organized naturalism' or 'anti-supernaturalism' seem to be rampaging triumphantly through the Church and the world today. Arm yourselves for the battle!

Loreto Publications intends to publish the following works of Fr. Denis Fahey:

Mental Prayer According to the Teaching of Saint Thomas Aquinas (1927)
The Kingship of Christ According to the Principles of Saint Thomas Aquinas
(1931)
The Mystical Body of Christ in the Modern World (1935)
* *The Rulers of Russia* (1938)
* *The Workingmen's Guilds of the Middle Ages* (1943)
(A translation of the work by Dr. Godefroid Kurth C.S.G.)
The Kingship of Christ and Organized Naturalism (1943)
* *Money Manipulation and the Social Order* (1944)
The Mystical Body of Christ (1945)
The Mystical Body of Christ and the Reorganization of Society (1945)
* *The Tragedy of James Connolly* (1947)
* *The Rulers of Russia and the Russian Farmers* (1948)
The Kingship of Christ and the Conversion of the Jewish Nation (1953)
The Church and Farming (1953)
The Duties of the Catholic State in Regard to Religion (1954)
(A translation of the work by Cardinal Alfredo Ottaviani)

* Currently available from Loreto

Editor's notes

Loreto's editions of the works of Father Fahey have been newly typeset and updated with some changes to the original text. The alterations are as follows:

1. We have changed the spelling of many words to match modern American spelling rules. Some examples are: neighbor for neighbour, show for shew, labor for labour, realize for realise, mold for mould, program for programme, etc.

2. We have made use of current punctuation and capitalization rubrics. 3. We have made a few minor corrections of typographical errors in the original texts but have NOT altered the words of Fr. Fahey nor made any deletions.

4. We have made uniform the notations of scripture references in the currently accepted fashion. For example, we use Mt. 24: 6–9 instead of Matt. xxiv 6, 7, 8, 9.

Biographical sketch of Father Denis Fahey, C.S.Sp.

(July 3, 1883 – January 21, 1954)

Denis Fahey was born in Golden, County Tipperary, Ireland, on the land and among kinsmen whom he dearly loved. The parish of Knockavilla where he was baptized is part of the Diocese of Cashel. He was, by the grace of God born into a devout Catholic family that was blessed with three sons. Thomas was the oldest. John died very young, and Denis was the youngest son of his parents, Thomas and Brigit (Cleary), who were deeply devoted to the Church. Denis was sent at the age of twelve to Rockwell College, where he was educated by the Holy Ghost Fathers among whom his vocation to the priesthood was nurtured and eventually came to fruition.

At the age of 17 he entered the novitiate of the Holy Ghost Fathers at Grignon-Orly, near Paris. He made his religious profession on February 2, 1907 and was ordained to the priesthood in Rome on September 24, 1910. The ordination was conferred by Cardinal Respighi at St. John Lateran.

Father Fahey's life work was the promotion of the Catholic social doctrine of Christ the King. He firmly believed that "the world must conform to Our Divine Lord, not He to it." He always defended the Mystical Body of Christ without compromise.

"See to it, Venerable Brethren, that the faithful do not allow themselves to be deceived! Communism is intrinsically wrong."

From the encyclical letter of Pope Pius XI,
Divini Redemptoris, on Atheistic Communism

CHAPTER ONE
DEMAND FOR MONETARY REFORM IN ENGLAND

The following letter was addressed in 1943 to His Excellency, Most Reverend William Godfrey, the Apostolic Delegate to Great Britain, to the Anglican Archbishops of Canterbury, York, and Wales, and to other ecclesiastical dignitaries in Great Britain. It was accompanied by a proposal to form an association having for object an honest national money system for England. The letter runs as follows:

Your Grace,

(1) We, all of British blood and descent, having studied the fundamental causes of the present world unrest, have long been forced to the conclusion that an essential first step towards the return of human happiness and brotherhood with economic security and liberty of life and conscience, such as will permit the Christian ethic to flourish again, is the immediate resumption by the community in each nation of its prerogative over the issue of money including its modern credit substitutes.

(2) This prerogative has been usurped by those still termed in general 'bankers,' both national and international, who have perfected a technique to enable themselves to create the money they lend by the granting of bookkeeping credits, and to destroy it by the withdrawal of the latter at their discretion, in accordance with entirely mistaken and obsolete ideas which they do not defend against impartial and informed scientific criticism and examination. In this way a form of national money debt has been invented, in which the lender surrenders nothing at all; and which it is physically an impossibility for the community ever to pay. Any attempt to do so produces the artificial 'economic blizzard,' as it did after the 1914–18 war.

(3) This has led to the gradual rise of a form of national, international and supra-national power, dominating through its monopolization of the national social credit all the basic creative activities of mankind. Thus, in this as in other countries, it has become impossible to obtain publication in the press, or to broadcast on the radio, the truth concerning this economic enslavement which holds the peoples of the world in thrall.

(4) Under the world's present financial system, the money, except for a now trifling proportion, is originally created by the issue of a loan at interest by the "bankers," who lend nothing themselves but in effect make a forced levy in kind on the nation by conferring on the borrower the power to purchase a corresponding amount of wealth on the market, which wealth does not belong to them, or those who borrow from them, but to the community. The proceeds of the issue of new money—whether of paper or any other form of credit money—belong to the nation in which it is, or is accepted as, legal tender, and not to the issuer. Herein lies the basic flaw of the existing monetary system.

(5) By this method, which has come to be regarded as legal by virtue of established practice, the banks in our country are responsible for the issue of new money of their own creation amounting today to between two and three thousand million pounds—this being the difference between loans extended, including those to themselves, and those repaid since they instituted the system a number of years ago and are thereby extracting by means of interest an annual tribute from the nation of over £100,000,000 for what has now become to them a relatively costless and risk-less service. But the real danger, well understood in every preceding era of history, is the undermining of all lawfully constituted authority by the creation and destruction of money carried on in secret for private gain and the acquisition of power.

(6) All forms of government, whether conservative, liberal or labor, fascist, socialist or communist, fall alike under the control of a political power group, which is ultimately, and in large measure unwittingly, dominated by the money creators and manipulators. In this way the national political power, which, if the individual is to enjoy the maximum of personal freedom consistent with his duty to his conscience and his fellows, should be distributed throughout the people, has been usurped without their knowledge or consent.

(7) It will be seen that the present monetary system, which by its disregard of primary physical and ethical laws is inevitably destroying the civilization into which it has been introduced, requires rectification both in its material technique and in the ethics which at present inspire and control this technique. It is particularly in view of its devastating effects in the moral sphere that we have ventured to refer to ecclesiastical authority, and to invoke the churches to action.

(8) We therefore appeal to you in your position of great authority and influence to proclaim the truth to the nation on this subject and in the hope that you may see fit to disseminate as widely as possible the text of this statement, whereby this vitally important question may be brought to the light of day and earnestly enquired into by the peoples of the British Commonwealth.

(9) We do so in all Christian fellow-feeling, knowing and honoring the efforts you are making against the abuses of our present economic system and the evils of usury, and believing that the world is now in the gravest crisis of its history. The issue of new money by the moneylender is an unforeseen result of the modern check as a substitute for national money—a valuable invention, which in itself was undoubtedly social and benevolent in intention and effect. If the check system were corrected, as it can be simply corrected, to restore to the nations their rightful prerogative over the issue of money, there is every reason to retain it. We fully appreciate the services which banking organizations have rendered and can continue to render to the community. But the issue and destruction of money by the moneylender is not a service, but a weapon which can be and has been used to perpetuate poverty amidst abundance, which renders individuals and nations powerless to protect themselves, and which may even be perverted to serve vast designs for the complete subjugation of the human race to tyranny, exploitation and the powers of darkness and evil.

NORMAN A. THOMPSON - (A.M.I.E.E., Research Engineer, Inventor of the Norman Thompson Flying Boat, 1914, and other developments in   aviation and in mechanical propulsion; originator of this appeal)

FREDERICK SODDY - (M.A., LL.D., F.R.S., Nobel Laureate in Chemistry, *1921;pioneer in the Economics of Wealth, author of Wealth,*

Virtual Wealth and Debt (1926), *Money versus Man* (1931), *Role of Money* (1934), etc.

THE REV. P. T. R. KIRK (Vicar of Christ Church, Westminster).

MAURICE RECKITT - (M.A., Editor of *Christendom, a Journal of Christian Sociology*; author of *Faith and Society*, 1932)

THE REV. P. McLAUGHLIN   (Warden of Saint Anne's House, Soho, London, W. 1)

J. CREAGH SCOTT - (D.S.O., O.B.E., Lt. Colonel; Chairman, The Farmers' Action Council; Advisory Chairman, The Service for Economic Action)

REGINALD ROWE - (Kt., President, Economic Reform Club and Institute, and of Nat. Fed. of Housing Societies; a Governor of the Old Vic and Sadler's Wells; author of *The Root of All Evil*)

JOHN HARGRAVE - (F.R.S.A.; inventor of the Hargrave Automatic Navigator for Aircraft (1937); Econ. Adviser to the Planning Comm. H.M. Govt. of Alberta (1936–7); Founder and Leader of the Social Credit Party of G.B.; author of *Summer Time Ends*, etc.)

ROBERT J. SCRUTTON - (Founder-President of the People's Common Law Parliament; Monetary and Constitutional Reformer to establish a Christian Social Order. Books: *A People's Runnymede*, *Let the People Rule*, etc.)

WILFRID HILL - (Industrialist, Birmingham and London; Pres., Comité International des Echanges, Paris; Chairman, Econ. and Monetary Joint Council, London; Anglo-American Committee World Trade Alliance)

GLYN THOMAS - (Manufacturer; author of *The Hour Sterling*)

CHARLES TURNER - (Mech. and Mining Engineer; Knowles Gold Medalist; inventor of the oil-from-coal process and plant)

CHRISTOPHER A BECKETT WILLIAMS -(Political Journalist)

ALLIOTT VERDON-ROE - (Kt., O.B.E., F.R.Ae.S., M.I.Ae.E.; pioneer of Aviation and Money Reform. Books: *Alberta is Fighting our War* (1937) *A World of Wings and Things* (1938); etc.)

L. B. POWELL - (Editor of *Cavalcade*)

R. R. STOKES - (Member of Parliament for Ipswich)

H. J. MASSINGHAM - (Author of *World Without End*, *The English Countryman*, *Remembrance*, etc.)

MRS. GLADYS BING - (Speaker and writer on Social Credit. Author of *The Fraud of Taxation*)

C. H. CLENDINING - (Founder and Chairman of The Ex-Service Party; North Atlantic Air Route Development; Chairman, Irish Trans-Atlantic Corp., Ltd., 1932–8)

I. V. ROBINSON - (M. Inst. C.E., M.I.Mech. E., Whitworth Scholar, M. Amer. S.M.E., F.S.S.; Hon. Treas. London Social Credit Club, etc.)

A. G. SEAMAN - (M.I.E.E.; inventor of Automatic Sorting of Heavy Goods)

B. D. KNOWLES - (Author of *Britain's Problem*)

A. ROMNEY GREEN (F.R. Econ.S.; Geometrician and Writer; Promoter for a Scheme for Minimum Incomes without state Regimentation; author of Rehabilitation of the Small Man, Christendom, 1943)

C. MARSHALL HATTERSLEY - (M.A., LL.B; Solicitor; author of *The Community's Credit* (1922) ; *This Age of Plenty* (1929); *Wealth, Want and War* (1937), and other works on social economics)

HENRY S. LAWRENCE - (K.C.S.I.; formerly Finance Minister of Council, Bombay Presidency, India; Member of Roy. Comm. on Agriculture (1926–'8) ; author of *Freedom from Fear and Want - Empire Review*, 1942)

W. D. CLARKE - (Farmer; author of *Why Prices of Agricultural Products Fluctuate*, 1936)

LADY CLARE ANNESLEY - (Speaker on Social Reform and Monetary Reform)

THE REV. J. CLIFFORD GILL - (Morecambe, Lanc.; author of *The Mastery of Money*)

W. J. BROWN - (Member of Parliament for Rugby; Parliamentary General Secretary of the Civil Service Clerical Assn.)

THE REV. C. H. LAMBERT - (Canon of Blackburn ; Warden of Whalley Abbey and Diocesan Director of Religious Education)

ARTHUR CUE - (Gas Engineer; author of *A Plan for a Scientifically and Morally Sound Currency*)

ANDREW MacLAREN - (Member of Parliament for Burslem)

In a covering letter, signed by Mr. Norman A. Thompson and Professor Frederick Soddy, it was stated that "if the way is not already paved before the cessation of hostilities towards a saner economic system under which all members of the nation will receive a more equitable and humane treatment, the return of our countrymen serving in the forces, who are becoming increasingly aware of the injustices of the existing monetary system, is likely to be the prelude to uncompromising disturbances."

As we in Ireland have been and are living under the same monetary system, some friends have done me the honor of inviting me to examine the reasons which have elicited this protest from so many distinguished English men and women.

Now, in the Encyclical Letter, *Studiorum Ducem*, on Saint Thomas Aquinas as "Guide of Studies", Pope Pius XI points out that Saint Thomas's philosophy and theology are so perfect that "he is our source for economic and political science." Accordingly, I shall begin by a brief exposition of the political, economic and financial principles of Saint Thomas Aquinas.

CHAPTER TWO

POLITICAL, ECONOMIC AND FINANCIAL PRINCIPLES
OF SAINT THOMAS AQUINAS

SAINT THOMAS AND POLITICS

Politics is the science which has for object the organization of the state in view of the complete common good of the citizens in the natural order and the means that conduce to it. As the final end of man is, however, not merely natural, the state, charged with the temporal social order, must ever act in such wise as not only not to hinder but to favor, the attaining of man's supreme end, the vision of God in three divine persons. Political thought and political action therefore, in an ordered state, will respect the jurisdiction and guidance of the Catholic church, the divinely-instituted guardian of the moral order, remembering that what is morally wrong cannot be politically good. Thus the natural or temporal common good will be always aimed at by those in authority in the way best calculated to favor family life, in view of the development of true personality, in and through the Mystical Body of Christ. Political action and legislation, especially in economic matters, must ever seek to strengthen family life and, accordingly, must not only not admit divorce, but must always aim, as far as possible, at benefiting citizens through their families.

SAINT THOMAS AND ECONOMICS

Etymologically, economy is the government of the home and the family. Economics is the science which studies the component cells of the state, namely, families, in the constituent relations of their members and in their conditions of existence. It aims at elucidating, *primarily*, the personal relations which constitute the family, the relations of husband and wife, parents and children, masters and servants, and then, *secondarily*, the relations that follow from the conditions of existence of the family, namely, the mutual relations of human persons arising from their need of external goods or real wealth. On the one hand, our nature brings us into relation with earthly resources which, by taking account of their nature and laws, we have to transform into real wealth capable of satisfying our corporal needs. Such are the relations of men with minerals, stone, lime, copper, iron, petrol; with the flora and fauna that people the earth, air and water; with the nerves and muscles of our own bodies. On the other hand, from this necessary utilization of things follow personal social relations between us: relations between cultivators of the soil and artisans, between employers and employed, between industrialists and merchants, between buyers and sellers. All these relations, however, are between human persons whose wellbeing is bound up with strong family life. Needless to say, the organization of family life, in view of providing its members with sufficient material resources, is, though secondary, a very important element of economics. As Saint Thomas points out, a sufficiency of material goods is necessary for the virtuous life of the average human being.'[1]

Economics, then, will study: firstly, the constituent relations of the members of Christ, who compose the family; secondly, the science of the production, distribution and exchange of natural wealth, in view of securing that sufficiency of material goods which is normally indispensable for the virtuous life of members of families; thirdly, the auxiliary art of the manipulation of money or artificial wealth, which is meant to facilitate families in procuring by exchange the above-mentioned sufficiency.

THE ROLE OF MONEY

According to right order, then, money or exchange medium is for the production of material goods, and the production of material goods is for the virtuous life of members of Christ of which the foundation is laid in the Christian family. Money, according to Saint Thomas, was invented by the art of man for the convenience of exchange by serving as a common measure of things saleable. " Natural wealth," he writes (Ia IIae, Q.2, a. i,

---

[1] "That a man may lead a virtuous life two things are required. The chief requisite is virtuous action, for virtue is that by which one leads a good life. The other requisite, which is secondary and quasi-instrumental in character, is a sufficiency of material goods, the use of which is necessary for virtuous action" (*De Regimine Principum*, Lib. I, Cap. XV).

c.), "is that by which natural wants are supplied, for example, food, drink, clothing, vehicles, dwellings and such like. Artificial wealth is that which is not a direct help to nature, as for instance, money. This was invented by the art of man, for the convenience of exchange by serving as a common measure of things saleable." As a common measure it ought to be *stable*. "As a measure used for estimating the value of things," writes St. Thomas (*Comment. in Ethic.*, Lib. V, Lect. IX), "money must keep the same value, since the value of all things must be expressed in terms of money. Thus exchanges can readily take place and, as a consequence, communications between men are facilitated." Money is, therefore, essentially an exchange medium. Stability in value is a property or necessary attribute of an exchange medium. Money is meant to facilitate families in procuring by exchange the sufficiency of material goods required for the virtuous life of the human personalities composing them. The virtuous life of human persons is simply their ordered development in supernatural life as members of Christ.

Accordingly, as practical sciences or arts are arranged in hierarchical order according to the hierarchical order of their ends, the art of the manipulation of money must be at the service of politics and economics. Those who are skilled in the manipulation of money must be the servants of the state, not the dictators of governmental policy; they must aim at aiding and strengthening family life, not at disrupting it for the sake of the figures in their ledgers. It is completely against order if the production and the distribution of the goods needed by families must conform to the exigencies of moneymaking instead of the other way round. If, by a perversion of the right order, money or exchange medium becomes the master, production and distribution will decay, the potentialities of the state's resources will not be realized, and family life will suffer. If the manipulators of money get control of the government of the state then the government will not be able to compel the bankers and the money changers to practice the virtue of social justice, namely, that justice which has for object the common good, and the welfare of the whole nation will suffer grievously. Usury and alteration of the price level will then be permitted to go unchecked, and the real sovereignty in the state will inevitably pass into the hands of the manipulators of money. The next stage will be a move to bring national sovereignty under the domination of some international organization subject to finance. That will make permanent and worldwide the present day anti-Christian and anti-natural perversion of order involved in the subordination of human persons to the production of material goods and in the subordination of the production and distribution of material goods to finance.

For Saint Thomas, it is the duty of the state to see that money or exchange medium is a stable measure of value. In other words, just as the state must maintain stable measures of weight and length, in view of commutative justice in buying and selling, so it must aim at stability of the price level, the price of a thing being the expression of its exchange value in terms of money. " It is true," writes Saint Thomas (*Comment. in Ethic.*, Lib. V, Lect. IX), " that it is the same with money as with other things, namely that one does not always get what one wants for it, because it is not always endowed with the same purchasing power, that is, it is not always of the same value. But, nevertheless, matters should be so arranged that it should be steadier in value than other things... As a measure used for estimating the value of other things, *money must keep the same value*, since the value of all things must be expressed in terms of money. Thus exchanges can readily take place and, as a consequence, communications between men are facilitated." [2]

---

[2] For a fuller treatment of the principles of Saint Thomas Aquinas concerning money, the reader is recommended to read *The Mystical Body of Christ and the Reorganization of Society,* Chapter III.

CHAPTER THREE

THE FUNCTIONING OF THE
GOLD STANDARD MONETARY SYSTEM

MONEY MANIPULATORS AND GOVERNMENTS

We have seen that for Saint Thomas money is meant to be the servant of politics and economics. The art of manipulating money or exchange medium must not be allowed to fall uncontrolled into the hands of private individuals, as they will be tempted to work for instability of price levels in view of their own gain. *A fortiori*, the rulers of the state must see to it that the manipulators of money do not get control of the government. Now these two evils—instability of national price levels and control of governments by financiers—seem to have been allowed to grow apace under the gold standard monetary system. We shall begin by some testimonies about the second point—the control of governments by financiers.

Let us take, first of all, a clear statement of principle by a well-known financier recently deceased, the Rt. Hon. Reginald McKenna, Chairman of the Midland Bank and former English Chancellor of the Exchequer. At the Midland Bank meeting of January, 1924, he said: " I am afraid that the ordinary citizen will not like to be told that the banks can, and do, create money. The amount of money in existence varies only with the action of the banks in increasing and decreasing deposits and bank purchases. Every loan, overdraft or bank purchase creates a deposit, and every repayment of a loan, overdraft or bank sale destroys a deposit. And they who control the credit of a nation, direct the policy of governments and hold in the hollow of their hands the destiny of the people." In his 1927 speech, the same distinguished banker said that the total of available bank cash on which the quantity of loans or deposits of private banks depended was determined by the Bank of England. Thus we can conclude that, according to this former

Chancellor of the Exchequer, the Governor of the Bank of England directs the policy of the English government and practically holds in his hands the destiny of the English people.

Let us now take the testimonies of the rulers of states. When the Federal Reserve Bank of the United States, created in 1913 by Mr. Paul Warburg, a German Jew belonging to the banking firm of Kuhn, Loeb and Company, had been a few years in existence, in 1916 to be precise, President Woodrow Wilson thus summed up the situation in U.S.A., "A great industrial nation is controlled by its system of credit. Our system of credit is concentrated. The growth of the nation, therefore, and all our activities are in the hands of a few men."

We have come to be one of the worst ruled, one of the most completely controlled and dominated governments in the civilized world—no longer, a government by conviction and the free vote of the majority, but a government by the opinion and duress of small groups of dominant men." From the similar testimonies quoted by Christopher Hollis in *The Two Nations*, let us take one. "Behind the ostensible government," ran Roosevelt's policy, "sits enthroned an invisible government owning no allegiance and acknowledging no responsibility to the people."[1]

If we pass to England, we shall find abundant evidence in proof of what Professor Soddy wrote about the Bank of England some years ago: "From being what is known as a banker's bank, it has become now almost the government's government." Mr. Gladstone said: "From the time I took office as Chancellor of the Exchequer (1852) I began to learn that the state held, in the face of the Bank and the City, an essentially false position as to finance. . . The hinge of the whole situation was this: the government itself was not to be a substantive power in matters of finance, but was to leave 'the money power' supreme and unquestioned. In the conditions of that situation I was reluctant to acquiesce, and I began to fight against it by financial self-assertion from the first . . . I was tenaciously opposed by the Governor and the Deputy-Governor of the Bank, who had seats in Parliament, and I had the City for an antagonist on almost every occasion." Mr. John Hargrave significantly adds in his book, *Professor Skinner alias Montagu Norman*: "It would astound the Grand Old Man to see the strides that the 'money power' has made in building and entrenching its position since his day."

---

[1] Op. cit., p. 219. *The Two Nations* is published by George Routledge and Sons, Ltd.

Mr. Hargrave also quotes Mr. Vincent Vickers, Bank of England director 1910–1919, as follows: "It was not Mr. Winston Churchill, as Chancellor of the Exchequer, who initiated or was to blame for our return to the gold standard in 1925; it was not Mr. Baldwin who decided the terms of the Bank Notes and Currency Act . . . 1928; nor later was it Lord Snowden who personally pigeonholed that request for a Royal Commission on monetary policy and who substituted so soon afterwards the McMillan Committee which seemed to some so redolent of Threadneedle Street. Since 1919 the monetary policy of the government has been the monetary policy of Mr. Montagu Norman." If we link with this the declaration already quoted from Mr. Reginald McKenna, distinguished banker and former Chancellor of the Exchequer, to the effect that "they who control the credit of a nation direct the policy of the government," we have reliable testimony as to the real ruler of England. In conclusion we may add to this that the Bank of England was empowered by the Income Tax Act of 1918, Section 68, to assess and tax itself with nobody in control. The Bank of Ireland was accorded the same privilege by the same (British) Act of 1918.

In point of fact, with the growing influence of American financial interests, power over the British government seems later to have passed to the other side of the Atlantic. Mr. Thomas Johnston, M.P., who in 1931 was Lord Privy Seal in the Labor government, wrote: "The City, the financiers and the moneylenders in New York and Paris, refused to put up credits in support of a balanced budget. They demanded a cut in unemployment benefit. They wanted humanity crucified on a cross of gold. We declined absolutely and resigned. . . Twenty men and one woman—a British Cabinet—waited one black Sunday afternoon in a Downing Street garden for a final decision from the Federal Reserve Bank of New York."[2]

The above will suffice to bring home to my readers the existence of a fundamental disorder in modern states, namely, the control of

---

[2] *Tax-bonds or Bondage,* by John Mitchell, p. 12. Christopher Hollis in *The Two Nations* (p. 241), says that the American financiers "made the reduction of the English dole a condition of their granting a loan of gold to the Bank of England . . . it is true that Mr. Ramsay MacDonald, as a general rule, pretended that it was not American dictation which was responsible for the reduction of the dole, but in a moment of forgetfulness he admitted that it was so in the House of Commons in answer to a question from Mr. Frank Owen." He quotes the text of Hansard, vol. 256, col. 1272 (21st Sept., 1931).

governments by those skilled in the manipulation of money or exchange medium. Finance is meant to be the servant of politics and economics. Instead it has come to be the master of both, so that human beings are sacrificed to the production of material goods and the production and distribution of material goods are sacrificed to finance. In the realm of production, as we shall see later, this disorder has led to the subordination of farming, by which the primary necessities of life are produced, to industry and the manufacture of secondary things. This reversal of order in regard to production is having disastrous consequences in soil erosion, loss of fertility, and ill-health of human beings, animals and living things in general.

Let us now turn to the evil of instability of price levels. This will need longer elaboration.

DEFECTIVE PRINCIPLES ADOPTED BY THE BANK OF ENGLAND WITH REGARD TO THE ISSUE OF MONEY

Money, as we have seen, has been invented to serve as a stable measure of exchange in view of facilitating families in procuring the material goods necessary for the virtuous life of the persons composing them. Material goods are produced by the application of the available labor to the resources of the country. Money or exchange medium is the indispensable means to enable this to be easily done in a complex society and thus permit the productivity of a country to be readily actualized. But the principle governing the injection of money into the country's industrial system must be the determination to actualize the country's potential resources in view of the common good. The endeavor must be to reach the point in which all the available labor and resources are being utilized in a manner respectful of the Catholic church's program of the widest possible diffusion of property. There has to be a planned gradual development, but the increasing capacity of a nation to make and supply goods ought never to be hampered by the lack of *the means* to carry on the indispensable exchanges. As money is, broadly speaking, a claim on the goods capable of being produced by the persons owning property in a community, its rate of issue must be regulated by the rate of actualization of these goods. The regulation of the issue of money on other principles will lead inevitably to a defective and lopsided development of a country's resources.

In the history of the Bank of England, we find the issue of money regulated by two very defective principles. The first of these is more or less clearly embodied in the Tonnage Act, or Bill of 1694, by which the Bank of England came into being almost by the back door. (The expression "almost by the back door" is that employed in the *Encyclopedia Britannica, 24th Ed.*, Vol. III, Article Bank of England, p. 53). The preamble reads: "A Bill for granting to their Majesties several Rates and Duties upon tonnages of Ships, Vessels, and upon Beer, Ale and other Liquors: for securing certain Recompenses and Advantages, in the said Bill mentioned, to such persons as shall voluntarily advance the sum of fifteen hundred thousand pounds towards carrying on the War against France." The chief of the "Recompenses and Advantages," which were granted to subscribers to the loan, who were to constitute a corporation to be known as "The Governor and Company of the Bank of England," was that the corporation was to have *the right to issue notes up to the volume of its total capital.* "The bank's capital was £1,200,000," writes G. B. Knowles in *Britain's Problem,* "the whole of which sum was to be advanced to the government at a rate of 8%, plus £4,000 *per annum* for expenses, or £100,000 *per annum* in all. The privileges of a bank were granted for twelve years to the corporation, which was allowed to deal in bills of exchange or bullion, but not in merchandise, and . . . to manufacture and issue notes up to a volume equal to that of its capital. To use William Paterson's own words: "The bank hath benefit of interest on all moneys which it creates out of nothing." When the bank's charter was renewed in 1709, the right was granted to double its capital and so its note issue.

Thus the issue of new money depended, not upon the rate of actualization of the country's resources, but upon the amounts borrowed from time to time by the government, and those borrowings were largely for foreign wars. This was the beginning of that phenomenon which has given rise to so much criticism since the Great War (1914–1918). Money is forthcoming in abundance for war but not for the peaceful development of the country. "The first advance," writes Mr. Belloc in his *Shorter History of England,* "had been just over a million. In four years the national debt was twenty millions, and in twenty years it was already over fifty millions. It became a permanent institution. In this fashion governments were enabled, for their purposes, to saddle posterity with the duty of financing their wars, whilst what was worse, wealthy men found the opportunity for levying a permanent tax on the community. If you had £10,000 to invest all you had to do was to buy government stock, and you were certain of getting your interest forever out of the taxpayers.

Another defective principle with regard to the issue of money was adopted by the Bank of England about 1783. In the *Rise of the London Money Market,* by W. R. Bisschop, on pages 168 and 169, we read: "Whilst in 1780 the value of the notes in circulation was about £6,500,000, this amount had risen to £9,500,000 in 1783. About this time the bank adopted the unfortunate theory that the note circulation should be contracted simultaneously with an efflux of gold from the bank, in order to bring about a reflux of the specie withdrawn . . . The author of this idea was Mr. Bosanquet." In a note the same author adds: "According to Mr.

Bosanquet the single fact sufficed that gold was withdrawn from the bank irrespective of the question whether it was required for internal circulation or for abroad."

It is quite clear that making the volume of money dependent on the volume of gold not only divorced the supply of money available in the country from any relation to the actualization of the country's productivity but by causing the amount of money to fluctuate was bound to prove disastrous for the stability of the price level. It is not necessary to elaborate the first point, as it is quite clear. The second point is excellently treated by Mr. Geoffrey Crowther in *An Outline of Money*. "The two functions of the gold standard," he writes, "are quite distinct." The first, aiming at control of the volume of note issue, is obviously concerned with the internal value of the currency; we may, therefore, call it the domestic gold standard. The second, aiming at the stability of the external value of the currency, we call the international gold standard . . . The cardinal point in the domestic gold standard is clearly the proportion of volume enforced by the law between the gold reserve and the currency. The essence of the international gold standard is the convertibility of the currency into gold—that is, the fixed proportion of value between a unit of gold and a unit of currency . . . Not only is a minimum gold reserve a wasteful way of regulating the volume of the currency, it is also a most capricious one. For it does not stabilize the volume of the currency, it merely stabilizes the relations between the volume of gold and the volume of the currency, and if the volume of gold is itself fluctuating, the domestic gold standard does not stabilize the volume of the currency but forces it to fluctuate . . . An expanding, progressive world needs an expanding supply of currency, and if the annual percentage increment to the gold stock does not equal the annual increase in the demand for currency there will tend to be either an excess or a deficiency of currency, and hence a tendency to rising or falling prices. This can be clearly seen from the monetary history of the nineteenth century." Since "pursuit of price stability is not compatible with maintenance of the gold standard," the principle adopted by the Bank of England about 1783 was in reality the abandonment by those manipulating the primary currency of the world of the essential property of an exchange medium.

Another evil arising out of the adoption of the domestic gold standard is that gold can be cornered and thus the power to seesaw prices in different countries will fall into the hands of a few men. It is bad enough to have to endure instability of prices owing to the action of what we may call natural causes on the supply of gold: it is the very reversal of order to have the well-being of the community, the common good, at the mercy of a few schemers, while the national government looks on helplessly. "Always remember," writes Miss G. M. Coogan in *Money Creators*, " that the price of an ounce of gold, in terms of the currency of any nation, is *purely arbitrary* it is fixed either by law, as in so-called fixed-conversion countries (U.S.A., Holland, France), or by open market bidding by the gold brokers (England, the Colonies, Argentine, etc.). . . Gold brokers, it is reported, meet daily in London at the office of the Rothschilds. The Rothschilds are very conveniently the agents for the Royal Mint. The following firms (in addition to N. M. Rothschild and Sons) appear to constitute the assembly of gold brokers: Samuel Montague and Co., 114 Old Broad Street, London, E. C.2 ; Mocatta and Goldsmid, 7 Throgmorton Ave., London, E.C.2; Pixley and Abell, Palmerston House, Old Broad Street, London, E.C.2; Sharpe and Wilkins, 19 Great Winchester Street, London, E.C.2. After England suspended gold payments in 1931 the gold brokers began to change the purely arbitrary price of an ounce of gold in London and in the British Colonies."

"Gold has been cornered, scrambled for, and hoarded," said the Rt. Hon. Winston Churchill in 1932. " It has risen enormously in price and the value of everything we have or earn has been diminished accordingly. This monstrous process has only to be continued long enough to shatter the civilization, as it has already broken the prosperity, of the world as we have known it."[3]

THE BANKER'S DISCOVERY

Given the defective principles of money manipulation outlined in the last section, it is easy to see how the financiers came to occupy their present dominant position in modern states. The bankers observed that about 90% of their total stock of gold remained in their vaults entirely undisturbed, and that only about 10% of the precious metal was required for the normal transaction of business. The banks then began to circulate far more promises to pay gold than they had gold to meet, and to collect interest on the fictitious money. The bankers "discovered that they could lend far more money than they possessed," writes Sir Reginald Rowe in *The Root of All Evil*, "that is to say, that they could issue far more promises to pay in gold than they could meet with all the gold of their coffers. This was

---

[3] Quoted in the introduction to *Tyranny of Gold*, by Hiskett.

because it was found in practice that the promised payments were never simultaneously demanded; in fact, except in crises, never more than one-tenth of these at any time."

What bankers had discovered was simply the working of the law of averages. Modern organization of money and banking depends almost entirely on the law of large numbers. If tokens were issued, say, to about a dozen people, one could never predict what would happen. The whole dozen might walk in and claim gold. But when one is dealing with millions of people the lodgments and withdrawals will tend to cancel out. Similarly a company could not insure only twelve people, for it could not predict their mortality; but it can make a good statistical prophecy about twelve thousand. In the days of the gold standard, "redeemability of notes could normally be kept up," writes Professor O'Rahilly in *Money*, "because though a number of people presented notes and obtained gold, a practically equal number presented gold and obtained notes. Thus it was not necessary to keep a gold backing for every note issued. It was sufficient . . . to keep a marginal amount, that is, sufficient to cover fluctuations about the average. . . If the redeemable tokens are issued on a sufficiently large statistical scale, the excess of withdrawals over lodgments in any period—and the excess of lodgments over withdrawals in some other period will be reduced to a small fraction of the total concerned. Moreover, these fluctuations will become regular and predictable. . . Thus it becomes quite safe . . . to issue redeemable tokens to which no gold corresponds." In other words, the goldsmiths or bankers found that they could not only lend nine-tenths of the gold originally entrusted to them but also that they could put into circulation, through 'creditworthy' borrowers, their own notes or receipts up to ten times the amount of these nine-tenths and yet be certain in practice of being able to pay out gold on demand for the proportion of notes presented at the cashier's desk. By the covering of 10% the bankers were always able to maintain the illusion that the whole of their notes and receipts were convertible into gold or were 'backed' by gold. "The successful maintenance of this illusion," writes Jeffrey Mark, whose explanation in *The Modern Idolatry* I have just summarized, "which depends essentially on the proportion of people in the community who, in practice, are likely to and do present their notes for gold redemption at the same time, is the 'convertible paper' and the 'sound' money of the modern banking system." "If we add to this fact," the same writer continues, "that these 'fictitious loans' (to borrow a convenient phrase from Prof. Soddy) were only granted against evidence of tangible security deposited with the goldsmith in an amount always in excess of the loan, and that this security was confiscated by the goldsmith if these 'loans' were not 'repaid' when called, we have an accurate picture in miniature of the modern financial system, under whose dictates we all necessarily live and suffer. Modern finance, even in the complicated medley of bugaboo which is carried on under the sounding titles of 'high finance' and 'international finance', is simply a vast elaboration and mystification based absolutely on these simple but mysterious principles."[4]

The toleration by the state of this practice of lending promises to pay to ten times the amount of money which the bankers had in their possession was the second and more important step in the bankers' advance to control in modern states. From the point of view of the ordinary man, and especially of the poor, it was the second and more fatal error. In point of fact, governments later on failed to realize that the so-called promises to pay, *i.e.* checks, had become money, in fact a far more important category of money than that issued by the state.

---

[4] *The Modern Idolatry* is published by Chatto and Windus, London.

CHAPTER FOUR
NATIONAL FINANCE AND THE GOLD STANDARD

Having seen the fundamental principles underlying the orthodox functioning of the gold standard, let us now examine the system at work in national finance. In the next chapter we shall see its effects on international trade.

Let us first examine the approximate figures of the various elements composing the medium of exchange in Great Britain, the country of origin of the gold standard system of finance. The figures are taken from page 55 of the excellent work already quoted, namely, *The Modern Idolatry*, by Jeffrey Mark. They are not meant by the author of this book, published in 1934, to set forth the exact amount in use, but to give a fairly accurate idea of the proportion which each kind of exchange medium bears to the others and to the whole amount. The actual figures may vary considerably, but the ratios between the categories remain substantially the same.

In Great Britain, out of £2,500 millions of exchange medium, approximately £10 million are in copper or bronze, £40 million are in silver, £450 million in Bank of England notes, and £2,000 million are what are called bank deposits. Bank deposits are really loans made by the banks and finally controlled by the central bank, in this case, the Bank of England. "Of the £450 million in bank notes some £250 million represent the British one pound and ten shilling Treasury Notes issued during the World War, which in 1928, under the terms of the Banknotes and Currency Act, came under the control and are now the virtual property of the Bank of England . . . . State issued money now consists entirely of the bronze (or copper) and silver coins, that is, about £50 million. The banks now own and claim as their property some £2,450 million out of £2,500 million. It is, therefore, clear that the British banks have created, except for about 2%, and now own, all the money in circulation in England, as a debt against the community. The situation in the U.S.A., and indeed in all civilized countries today, is substantially the same." Before we pass on, a remark must be made about the use of the word 'own' in the above quotation from Mr. Jeffrey Mark. "Controls or administers" would be more accurate. Professor O'Rahilly treats of the point on pp. 70–148 and again on p. 358 of his invaluable work, *Money*.

In 1934, therefore, about 98% of the money of Great Britain was controlled by the banks. We need not make any distinction from this point of view between notes and bank deposits, for whether on the presentation of security £1,000 is credited to a man's account in a bank ledger and he writes checks against it, or he obtains that bank's own notes for £1,000 and spends them, a 'deposit' has been created or an 'advance' made, and money or exchange medium has been brought into being. Notes give a clearer impression of new exchange medium being put into circulation; that is all. " What is created in the first instance," writes D. V. Maxwell in *The Principal Cause of Unemployment*, "is a bank deposit or what is called a 'deposit.'

For instance, if Mr. X obtains an 'advance' of £50 against security on Dec. 30 and does not spend it, the bank balance sheet of Dec. 31 will include the following items among many similar items:—

Liabilities	Assets
Deposit of Mr. X—£50	Advance to Mr. X—£50

A bank 'deposit' has been created.[1]

"There is no economic difference," writes Professor O'Rahilly in *Money*, "between those two methods (notes and checks) of creating new purchasing money. There would be no difference at all if, instead of giving the customer a book of blanks to be filled up as required, the banks were to issue a block of coupons of denominations such as 10s., £1, etc. As things are, there is merely a slight juridical distinction between a bank note and a check; a note is an absolute obligation to pay; a check is a contingent obligation, it may be dishonored if the customer has overdrawn beyond his agreement. . . . Hence there is no real social or economic difference between (1) a bank of issue which creates new purchasing power by the emission of notes and, (2) a bank of deposit which creates new purchasing power by the issue of credit transferable by check. The confusion of thought is chiefly due to the persistence of the word 'deposit' which no longer means *depositum*, but a debt."

These points must be insisted upon because of the mistaken idea that people have that "the function of the banker is, firstly, to take care of 'their'

---

[1] *The Principal Cause of Unemployment* is published by Williams & Norgate, Ltd., London.

money, and, secondly, to make profits by lending 'their' money to other people at a higher rate of interest that they themselves allow on deposits or on checking accounts. In the true sense of the word, the public do not own any money at all, and the phrase 'bank deposit' is a legal euphemism. Seeing that all money comes into existence as a debt created in favor of the banking system of the world, the plain truth is that bankers must always lend their own (created) money however much it may be criss-crossed between private 'debtors' and 'creditors' subsequently. No one has really any money to lend to the bankers on 'deposit' because all money 'owned' by depositors derives from a loan made by the banks to somebody else .... Yet the line taken by bankers, when publicly explaining any new move in policy, is that they have done so to protect their depositors' money . . .. The situation is simply this: Seeing that all credit is created by bank loans, for every 'deposit' in a bank, there is an equivalent loan somewhere else in the banking system, so that the total of 'deposits' is equal to the totality of the bank loans . . .. The amount of money in existence is increased if the aggregate of loans granted is greater than the aggregate of loans repaid or called in (credit expansion). It is decreased if the aggregate of loans granted is less than the aggregate of loans called in or repaid (credit contraction) . . .. Now the extent to which a bank can make loans is determined by its 'cash' holdings, which, in England, varies with the amount of its balance at the Bank of England, as the Rt. Hon. Reginald McKenna, the able Chairman of the Midland Bank, laid down at a meeting of the Midland Bank Shareholders (in 1927): 'Variations in the quantity of money are due to variations in the total of bank cash . . .. The total of bank cash is determined solely by the action of the Bank of England.' The authority of the Bank of England in fixing the amount of money in England is therefore absolute. The genesis of all inflations and deflations of the currency comes from a private corporation whose policy is not controlled by Parliament."[2]

Before passing on to speak of the evils of inflation and deflation, it will be well to explain the meaning of the phrase used above, namely, that "variations in the quantity of money are due to variations in the total of bank cash." Briefly it means that, as bankers are accustomed to lend promises-to-pay up to ten times the amount of legal tender money which they either possess or can count upon securing in case of a 'run' upon them, bankers' loans vary with the amount of their available legal tender money. A banker's balance sheet shows how much legal tender money he can count upon under the heading 'Cash and deposits at the central bank.'

---

[2] *The Modern Idolatry*, by Jeffrey Mark.

Cash is the amount of legal tender money he has actually in his possession. Deposits at the central bank are the credit balance of the private bank at the central bank. Deposits at the central bank are reckoned as cash because they can be immediately converted into legal tender money. The central bank will see to that.

There is one very important difference between cash and deposits at the central bank. Cash is legal tender money. Deposits at the central bank are a credit balance at the central bank, for which legal tender money can be obtained. The central bank by what are called 'open-market operations,' can increase or decrease the private bank's available supply of legal tender money, on which it has lent ten times the amount. When the central bank buys securities in the open market, it pays for them by checks drawn on itself. "The sellers of these securities lodge these checks to their credit in their own banks thus increasing their own deposits. The banks pass these checks into the central bank, thus increasing their balance at the central bank . . .. Hence the central bank by its 'open-market operation' has increased the cash ratio of the banking system. And it is easy to see that if the central bank sells securities (instead of buying them) it decreases the cash ratio of the banks as a whole." Hence the central bank can control the lending powers of the private banks and increase or decrease the amount of exchange medium in the country. The central bank is controlled by the movements of gold when the gold standard is functioning. An export of gold forces the central bank to reduce the credit balances of the private banks. Those who wish to study these questions further will find these brief explanations developed in *Promise to Pay* by R. McNair Wilson and *Money* by Professor O'Rahilly.'[3]

THE MEANING OF INFLATION AND DEFLATION

We have seen that by far the greater part, in fact all except (less than) 2%, of the exchange medium in use in Great Britain comes into existence as a loan from the banks, in the form of promises-to-pay. We may say, then, that the exchange medium of that country is practically created by the banks and that the rate of its creation is regulated by the private corporation called the Bank of England. "Instead of lending notes," writes Professor Soddy in *The Role of Money*, "the banks, in effect, now lend check books and the right to draw checks up to limited sums beyond what the borrower possesses. For nearly a century, until the revelations of the war

---

[3] *Promise to Pay* is published by George Routledge & Sons, Ltd. Money is published by the Cork University Press.

made it impossible to conceal the truth from the general public, the bankers stoutly denied that they were creating any money at all, and claimed that they were merely lending the deposits their clients were not using. The president of the Bank of Montreal not a year ago continued to repeat this, but, nearer the center of things, all this was known and admitted by the orthodox apologists for this monstrous system even before the war, usually by some such lying phrase as, 'Every loan makes a deposit.' A loan, if it is a genuine loan, does not make a deposit, because what the borrower gets, the lender gives up and there is no increase in the quantity of money, but only an alteration in the identity of the individual owners of it. But if the lender gives up nothing at all, what the borrower receives is a new issue of money and the quantity is proportionately increased. So elaborately has the real nature of this ridiculous proceeding been surrounded with confusion by some of the cleverest and most skilful advocates the world has ever known, that it still is something of a mystery to ordinary people, who hold their heads and confess they are 'unable to understand finance.' It is not intended that they should."

Let us now examine the alternate periods of boom and depression known as the Trade Cycle or Credit Cycle. During the opening stage, money is increased by the fact that more bank loans are made than are repaid. This causes a rise in prices and a corresponding diminution in purchasing power in the money already in the hands of people. This happens because the amount of exchange medium is increased before goods are ready to be exchanged, in consequence of its being left to private individuals, frequently mere speculators, to decide how much money shall go into circulation. Their aim, of course, is not to keep the price level stable, while enabling the potential productivity of the country to be developed, but to make profit for themselves. During the first stage, employment increases, producers and traders take loans. There is an increasing demand for goods. Prices continue to rise until purchasers at home, whose salaries and incomes have not risen in proportion, begin to buy abroad. This they can do by shipping gold instead of goods, for the price of gold is fixed and has not risen. But the moment gold begins to leave the country the bankers fear for their solvency, so they do not renew their loans when they are repaid. Money is thus withdrawn from circulation and the second stage of failing prices begins.

The loans contracted when prices were rising have now to be paid back when prices are falling—borrowers have to sell far more goods in order to obtain the same quantity of money to pay the banks—so a number of traders go bankrupt. Their securities are sold up by the banks or held until later, when another boom will enable them to be disposed of advantageously. The speculators sell when prices are still high, that is, if they are 'in the know,' and then wait before buying again till prices have fallen to the lowest level. A period of depression sets in and continues till the central bank, the Bank of England, gives the signal for a new series of loans by buying securities. That action gives the sellers' bank a credit balance at the Bank of England. Thus that bank, having more 'cash' at the central bank, can create more ledger money. A new credit cycle begins and follows the same disastrous course as the former. The rise of prices in the first stages swindles all creditors for the benefit of debtors. The fall of prices in the second swindles all debtors for the sake of creditors.

Ordinary people have a difficulty in following all this, because they always think of the bankers as lending money or exchange medium that has an existence independent of the banker's fiat. "What is not generally realized about the 'Credit Cycle,'" writes R. McNair Wilson in *Promise to Pay*, " is that the bankers are making profits both ways, by compelling buyers to pay them tribute during the booms and by compelling sellers to pay them tribute during the slumps—and all this by means of loans of promises-to-pay what none of them possessed—money." Ordinary people seem to have accepted, as they are meant to do, the explanation that all these cycles are the working of the law of nature. They will do well to read the interesting speeches put into the mouths of bankers and others by Miss G. M. Coogan in *Money Creators* (p. 28) and R. McNair Wilson in *Promise to Pay*.

According to Miss Coogan, the strong-room keeper, speaking at a meeting summoned to inquire into the cause of depression, in a sad voice told the committee that he regretted more than anyone in the community that the laws of economics were so rigid and did place such burdens on mankind, particularly on the weaker members of the community. It made him very sad to see under nourished and poorly clad children . . . but man did not make the laws of economics and he, as a guardian of the community's money, could do nothing else but recognize those bitter laws. There was simply no solution for the problem except economy. . . The community would have to face its problems courageously and they would simply have to economize more until the people either paid what they owed or surrendered their property. That was the only sound solution. They certainly had no desire to violate the laws of economics."

According to R. McNair Wilson, the banker waxes more lyrical about the laws of nature: "This movement of prices up and down," he declares, "is inherent in human nature. It belongs, too, to the nature of things as well as to the nature of men. Look at the seasons. Out of Winter darkness emerges the sunlight of Spring . . .. But all too soon the days begin to draw in. . . Never forget that a banker's first duty is towards his clients,

38

the honest and frugal folk who have entrusted to him the savings of their lifetime . . .. Would you have him make use of your savings to attempt to change the laws of nature, to try to sow in the time of reaping? . . .. There is no financial conjuring trick, believe me, which can change by an iota that law of nature, that economic law, that inexorable economic law."[4]

SOME HISTORICAL EXAMPLES OF PLANNED DEFLATIONS

The first example will be taken from the monetary system of the U.S.A. as outlined by Miss Coogan in her splendid book, *Money Creators*. She writes as follows: " Just one week after President Cleveland was inaugurated, the 'Panic Circular' was issued, March 12th, 1893. It appealed to the bond-holding classes to 'advocate an extra session of Congress for the repeal, unconditionally, of the Sherman Silver Law.' It was issued directly from the American Bankers' Association and addressed to all 'National Banks' throughout the U.S.A." Miss Coogan then continues "The following is a direct quotation from a resolution introduced to the 63rd Congress, First Section, April 29th, 1913, by Hon. Charles A. Lindberg, Sen.— "In eighteen hundred and ninety-three a circular was sent out by the American Bankers' Association, an organization in which most bankers hold membership. It is known as the 'Panic Circular of eighteen hundred and ninety-three' . . . and it was *mailed* to the National Banks. It read as follows:

Dear Sir:—The interests of national banks require immediate financial legislation by Congress. Silver, silver certificates, and Treasury notes must be retired, and National Bank notes on a gold basis [the phrase 'gold basis' always means a debt basis] made the only money. This will require the authorization of $500,000,000 to $1,000,000,000 of new bonds (debts) as the basis of circulation. *You will at once retire one-third of your circulation (your paper money) and call in one-half of your loans. Be careful to make a monetary stringency among your patrons, especially among influential businessmen.* Advocate an extra session of Congress to repeal the

---

[4] " The whole of that region (i.e., The East End of London)," wrote *The Times* at the time of the 1866 bank crash, is covered with huge docks, shipyards, manufactories and a wilderness of small houses, all full of life and happiness in brisk times but in dull times withered and lifeless, like the deserts we read of in the East. Now their spring is over. There is no one to blame for this it is the result of nature's simplest laws." This is quoted by Christopher Hollis in *The Two Nations* (p. 102).

purchasing clause of the Sherman Law, and act with other banks of your city in securing a large petition to Congress for its unconditional repeal per accompanying form. Use personal influence with your Congressmen and *particularly let your wishes be known to your Senators*. The future life of national banks, as fixed and safe investments, depends upon immediate action as there is an increasing sentiment in favor of governmental legal tender notes and silver coinage."[5]

The second example of the functioning of the 'economic law' of alternate boom and depression will be taken from the recent monetary history of Great Britain. In regard to this example we are particularly favored, for eight years before the 'coup' took place, Mr. Arthur Kitson foretold that it was being prepared. In his book, *A Fraudulent Standard*, published by King and Son, in 1917, we read: "Just now a few great financiers are contemplating the most gigantic 'deal' that has probably ever been conceived, and one which if perpetrated by any other class of the community even on a very much smaller scale would be denounced as barefaced robbery . . .. This deal is nothing less than doubling the national, and incidentally, all other debts, by doubling the present value of our monetary units. The object of this is to double the present value of their War Loan Investments, regardless of the terribly disastrous industrial and social results which must ensue. This robbery will be accomplished, if it is not checked in time by public sentiment, in a perfectly legal manner by a complacent Chancellor under the guise of a measure for the public welfare, for the sole purpose of removing 'inflation' and reducing prices that have risen mainly through the creation of the very currency and credit constituting the War Loans. The measure will aim at restoring what money dealers term our 'good, sound, honest gold currency,' by destroying the Treasury notes and reducing bank credit to the pre-war proportions. The effect will naturally be to double the purchasing power of the pound at the expense of every wage earner, producer, merchant, manufacturer, tradesman, and taxpayer in the country . . .. Nominally, of course, the amount of the war debt will undergo no change. The figures will remain the same . . .. By altering the value of the pound, which is easily accomplished, the trick is done and the debt, although nominally £6,000,000,000, becomes in reality £12,000,000,000 in terms of the present purchasing power of money, corresponding to the money actually on loan: similarly, although the normal rate of interest is 5%, by this method of tampering with the value of the pound, these investors will actually receive 10% on their original investment . . .. This will mean that every taxpayer will have to give at least twice the amount

---

[5] The additions in brackets are from the pen of the Hon. C.A. Lindberg.

40

of his goods and labor to meet his taxes, than that which he has had to furnish under present conditions."

In *The Bankers' Conspiracy*, pages 25–27, Mr. Kitson touches briefly upon the results of the re-establishment of the gold standard, foretold by him in 1917. "This document (*The Cunliffe Currency Committee's Report*)," he writes, " advised the adoption of certain monetary policies which were accepted by the coalition government of Mr. Lloyd George in 1920, under the Chancellorship of Mr. (now Sir) Austen Chamberlain, and is directly responsible for the most disastrous period in the industrial history of this country. Notwithstanding the ruinous results of the deflationary policy recommended in this report during the years immediately following its adoption, Mr. Winston Churchill intensified these evils by establishing the gold standard in 1925, which precipitated the great strike of 1926... The gold standard, re-established in 1925, after inflicting untold losses upon our industrial classes and taxpayers, had to be abandoned six years later to save the country from ruin. The same policies as those recommended by the Committee, have also been tried in other countries since the war and with similarly ruinous results hence the present world crisis. By the universal adoption of the gold standard after its recommendation by the Cunliffe Committee, which was one of the main policies advocated by the League of Nations, an irresponsible super-government was created, composed of a group of International Bankers. It required only a few years to prove the utter incapacity of these men to manage the world's financial affairs, and if the people of all civilized countries are not yet convinced of the terrible dangers attending the supremacy of the banking interests, there will be a repetition of the economic disasters of the last few years—but of a much more intensive character."

"We have to remember," writes Mr. Vincent C. Vikers, former director of the Bank of England, in *Finance in the Melting Pot* (p. 20), "that the value—that is to say, the purchasing power—of money, and consequently the price of goods, can be and has been varied intentionally and deliberately, not by the will or action of the state, but by those individuals who themselves manage and control the money—though they constantly aver that they act for, and on behalf of, the community. We returned to the gold standard in 1925 for the benefit of the City of London, and so ruined our basic industries. It does not follow that what is best for the City of London is best for the country.

"In consequence of past policy, a farmer who borrowed from his bank, say, in 1920, the money equivalent of 100 sacks of wheat, might be obliged to sell 200 sacks of wheat a few years afterwards in order to repay that same loan, simply because a pound became twice as valuable.

"This is typical of the 'gold standard system,' which involves inflation and deflation. A monetary system, which begets such flagrant injustice, cannot be regarded as an equitable system. Yet no one in authority here dares to attempt to alter it, because the financiers don't want it altered."

According to Christopher Hollis in *The Two Nations* (p. 232), "Mr. Winston Churchill claimed that the return to gold was no more responsible for the troubles in the mining industry (in 1926) than was the Gulf Stream." "But," he adds, "all serious students agreed with Mr. Keynes in dismissing the argument as 'feather-brained.'" At any rate Mr. Churchill thought differently in 1932. According to *The Standard* (Dublin), July 14, 1944, he said in the House of Commons on April 21, 1932: "When I was moved by many arguments and forces in 1925 to return to the gold standard, I was assured by the highest experts, and our experts are men of great ability and of indisputable integrity and sincerity, that we were anchoring ourselves to reality and stability, and I accepted their advice. I take for myself and my colleagues of other days, whatever degree of blame and burden for having accepted their advice.

"But what happened? We have had no reality, no stability. The price of gold has risen since then by more than seventy percent. That is as if a 12-inch foot rule had been stretched to 19 or 20 inches, as if the pound avoirdupois had suddenly become 23 or 24 ounces instead of 16.

"Look at what this has meant to everybody who has been compelled to execute their contracts upon this irrationally enhanced scale. Look at the gross unfairness of such distortion to all producers of new wealth, and to all that labor and science and enterprise can give us. Look at the enormously increased volume of commodities which have to be created in order to pay off the same mortgage debt or loan.

"Minor fluctuation might well be ignored, but I say quite seriously that this monetary convulsion has now reached a pitch where I am persuaded that the producers of new wealth will not tolerate indefinitely so hideous an oppression . . ..

"I therefore point to this evil, and to the search for the methods of remedying it as the first, second and third of all the problems which should command and rivet our thoughts."

CHAPTER FIVE
INTERNATIONAL TRADE AND THE GOLD STANDARD

From what has just been said about the organization of national finance under the gold standard, it can be easily seen that the system will not work satisfactorily in the realm of international trade. It inevitably leads to a state of affairs where every country wants to export goods in order to have a favorable balance of trade and where no country wishes to import. As, however, the exports of one nation are the imports of another, this leads to a deadlock. Sir Reginald Rowe sets forth the reason for this absurd situation briefly and clearly : "If we consider the International gold standard system, we shall see that it did not ensure an exchange of goods and services between nations to their mutual advantage but, on the contrary, ensured that nations should export their real wealth that is, goods and services, and obtain in return an admission of unpayable debt; the debt was supposed to be payable in gold and was called a' favorable 'balance, but if gold was, in fact, paid, the loss caused internal disaster to the country which paid it. Herein lies the reason, on the international side, why nations are so anxious to export and not import, although there is another internal reason connected with employment and the distribution of internal purchasing power through wages; the latter is also a monetary problem. . ..This country [England] for nearly 80 years had an annual so-called active 'favorable' balance of approximately £100,000,000. This meant that after it had paid all its bills to the world for all the imports and services it required, it still had £100,000,000's worth of foreign currencies owing to it.

Let us suppose, for the sake of simplicity, that the Argentine owed England annually the whole of this amount. England was then in a position to say to the Argentine : 'We have bought and paid for all the meat and wheat we required from you during the last accounting period, and after doing so we still have 100,000,000's worth of pesos for which we have no use. We can, if you like offer them for sale on the foreign exchange. If we do, some English exchange broker will give us pounds for them, but clearly as there is no immediate demand by Englishmen for them, no Englishman will give us their normal exchange value. He will expect to get more of them for his pound than the par value. In other words, if we offer these pesos for sale it will knock down your exchange rate. When it falls to the point where the loss in exchange would be greater than the loss represented by having to pay freight and insurance on the transport of physical gold, we shall cease selling pesos and go to the Central Bank of the Argentine and buy bars of gold; we shall ship them physically to England and sell them to the Bank of England and so get our pounds that way. When, however, the Central Bank of the Argentine loses gold to us, it will be obliged to take out of circulation paper pesos to a corresponding value. This will mean that the commercial banks will find themselves with less cash and, in order to maintain the same relationship of their loans to their cash, will be obliged to call in loans. This will mean that Argentine producers, manufacturers and merchants, will be obliged to throw their stocks on an unwilling market in order to raise the money to repay their bank loans. The throwing of these stocks on the market will have the effect of knocking down prices. It will be necessary for you to try to reduce wages as with lower prices you will not be able to afford to pay the same rate of wages as before. This will lead to strikes, and in any case, will destroy the purchasing power of the Argentine market.'

"The Argentine would reply, 'But this is terrible,' to which England was in a position to answer, ' Yes, devastating, and there is only one way out of the difficulty and that is that you borrow £100,000,000's worth of pesos at interest so as to take them out of harm's way. There will then be only due from you the annual interest. Next year, however, there will probably be another £100,000,000 which you will similarly have to borrow plus the interest on this year's £100,000,000.' In 14 years at 5 % compound interest each £100,000,000 would double itself. It will thus be seen that under the system, the Argentine was given the choice of getting hopelessly into debt to England or of losing gold with devastating effects."[1]

---

[1] *The Root of All Evil* is published by the Economic Reform Club, 32, Queen's Avenue, Muswell Hill, London, N. 10.

There is another side to this question, namely, the side of the people induced to invest in foreign enterprises. Interest is paid on these loans only to the extent that the creditors make further advances to enable the borrowers to do so. Christopher Hollis treats the point excellently: " Every year with but few exceptions, if you count in our invisible exports such as shipping and other services, we had a favorable balance of trade; every year we gave away more than we received. Therefore it is evident

The kernel of the difficulty of international trade under the gold standard system is that when a country's imports exceed its exports, the banks are liable to be asked for gold to cover the deficit. The reason is that the exchange will go against the country whose exports are down. At a certain point it will come to be more advantageous for those who have to pay debts in another country to buy gold, the price of which is fixed, and ship it to the other country to buy the exchange medium of that country. The export of gold will prevent the further fall of the exchange. For example, at one time, $4.86 bought one pound in the foreign exchange market, for each was worth the same amount of gold. If English exports to the U.S.A. came to exceed greatly English imports from the same country, there would be a great demand for pounds sterling and the cost of the pound in terms of dollars would gradually rise. When it reached $4.90, the difference between $4.86 and $4.90 would cover the cost of freight, insurance and loss of interest on gold. When gold could thus be bought and shipped, no one would pay more than $4.90 for a pound and the exchange would remain stable. Gold would be shipped in the opposite direction if the pound fell to about $4.84.

But the 'drain of gold' as it is called, will have a disastrous effect on the gold-exporting country. "Since International Bankers like Home Bankers, are lending promises-to-pay ten times the quantity of money they actually possess, it is obvious that strict limits are set to the export of gold . . .. In fact the International Bankers protect themselves by refusing to lend and trying to call up as many as possible of their existing loans—just as, in similar circumstances, the Home Bankers do." The results are that prices fall and the country tries to sell goods at a loss, while taking steps to recapture export trade by cutting down wages and dismissing workmen. Low wages mean the possibility of big exports. This means a lowering of the standard of living, especially of the wage earners. "The people whom international finance is playing off against each other," writes R. McNair

---

that last year's foreign investor, who thought he was this year receiving his dividend from his foreign investment, was not really doing so at all. He was really living on the savings of this year's foreign investor, who in his turn was to live on the savings of next year's foreign investor, and so on and so on, until the system's final and inevitable collapse .... Our exports visible and invisible, every year considerably exceeded our imports and there was a surplus left over for foreign investment. What in truth regulated the quantity of goods which we sold abroad was the quantity of loans which our financiers saw fit to make to foreigners to enable them to buy those goods" (*The Two Nations*, pp. 95, 115).

Wilson in *Promise to Pay*, "are not merely the merchants and industrialists of the world. The wage earners in every country are being pitted against the wage-earners in every other country. The attack on wages is everlasting and it is conducted by means of the wage earners themselves who have nothing to hope for unless they can produce cheaply, that is to say, unless they will accept lower wages than all their competitors . . .. The men, naturally, blame their masters; the masters blame their men. Both are helpless in the hands of the International Bankers since it is they who control the quantity of money in their markets . . .. If wages are not cut, half the businesses will be bankrupt. And when wages have been cut the whole hideous cycle will begin once more. Is it any wonder that, in such circumstances, Communism and Socialism, both will-o-the-wisps, flourish? Is it any wonder that class is set against class? Master against men? Nation against nation? Nobody suspects the true enemy."

The whole tendency of the system, then, is to lower the standard of living, since a country with a lower standard of living or low wages will be able to export. It is true that the gold standard keeps the value of money of any country stable in terms of foreign currencies, but this is only another way of saying that it tends to prevent wages in any country from remaining high when wages anywhere else fall. The net result is a dreadful struggle for the necessaries of life in the midst of potential sufficiency, the struggle being made far more tragic by gambling in the different currencies and speculation on the stock exchanges of the world.

A striking example of gambling in currencies is given by Mr. Arthur Kitson in *The Banker's Conspiracy*. He writes: "Some years ago *The Banker's Magazine* gave a startling example of the depreciation in the prices of 325 of our representative investments, caused by the withdrawal of £11,000,000 in gold from the Bank of England by a group of American financiers. The transfer of this amount caused a fall of prices equivalent to £115,000,000. The absorption of the same gold caused a corresponding advance in the prices of certain American securities. By first selling English securities and then buying American, they had merely to transfer so much gold and afterwards reverse the transactions by buying and selling respectively and the game was won! As a well-known financial writer stated at the time: 'These speculators were playing upon two tables at the same time—one in London and the other in New York—with the certainty of winning on both.'"

Let us now examine a little more profoundly the reason for the urge to export goods, which every country experiences, in spite of the fact that many under-nourished and ill-clad people in almost every country lack the very goods that are being exported or the goods into which they could be converted.

"Plenty of wool and no markets," announced a Dublin daily paper some time ago. "Plenty of poor and no blankets," was the very opposite comment of the humorous journal, *Dublin Opinion*.

The ultimate reason for the urge to export is to be found in the fact that 98% of all the money in existence comes into being with a demand for interest at five percent attached to it. We have already seen that in 1934 bank created money in Great Britain was over 98% while state created money was less than 2%. Now, "no more money can come out of the system than is put into it. If a certain proportion of businesses manage to pay back both principal and interest of their loans, the possibility or actuality of bankruptcy is automatically intensified for the whole of the remainder." The payment of the interest of money brought into existence as a debt involves the payment of more than is issued. This cannot be done without further borrowing, so the process means steady progression into debt for the society as a whole. It necessarily means also that, in every business cycle, a certain amount of the goods produced in that cycle remains un-purchased. This un-purchased surplus is increased by the fact that certain individuals in the society save up and re-invest their savings. Thus, as industry develops thanks to more and more loans, there is an ever-increasing surplus remaining un-purchased within the area of the society, and there is an ever-increasing demand for foreign markets. Debts, however, increase much faster than production, and production increases far more rapidly than distribution; so the urge to send goods abroad is accompanied by a proportionately increasing inability on the part of the inhabitants of the home-country to profit by the developing production. "The inevitable result of a financial system based on usury," writes Mr. Jeffrey Mark, "is the progressive accumulation of debt and a complementary decrease in the ratio between consumption and production. Between 1922 and 1929, for instance, debt claims in the United States increased 76%, against an increase in manufactured output of only 33%, and the distribution of consumer goods only 4%" The standard of living was raised but not at a rate commensurate with the increase in production.

Accordingly, the inevitable condition of foreign trade under the gold standard system is that every industrially developed nation must strive to export more than it imports. " If some nations have ' favorable' balances of payments," we read in *A Twentieth Century Economic System*, "other nations must have 'unfavorable' ones. International trade has therefore degenerated into financial war, instead of being an exchange of goods and services to the mutual advantage of both parties."

THE URGE TO WAR AND DESTRUCTION

It is unnecessary to dwell at length on the way the system we have described impels towards war. As practically every nation is suffering from "over production" and is trying to get rid of a 'surplus,' which its own impoverished thousands cannot purchase, the success of one nation in exporting means the intensification of the difficulties of another. Hitherto what was termed 'industrial progress,' along the lines indicated, could be maintained by the exploitation of 'backward' nations. But now the once 'backward' nations have themselves a 'surplus' to export. A terrible struggle for control of the remaining partially developed countries and a state of tension, which the armament manufacturers view with a glowing gratification because of *their* particular 'surplus stocks,' are inevitable."[2]

War means wholesale *indiscriminate* destruction, but peace, too, under the present monetary system means wholesale *systematic* destruction. Why is this? Because thus the prices of the remaining stocks will be raised, it is hoped, and the producers will be enabled to meet some of the interest claims on their debts. We have seen that production and distribution of real wealth are tolerated in so far as they facilitate the payment of interests on debts. Production and distribution which threaten to interfere with such payments cannot be allowed. Tariffs and quotas and the formation

---

[2] To Catholic students of history I would strongly recommend p. 217 in *The Two Nations*, by Christopher Hollis. " It was mainly into the countries of Spanish America," he there writes, "that American capital found its way. Some of it went there for those countries' economic development; other loans were political. For these latter there was almost a regular formula. It would be suggested to General X that he should raise a revolution against President A. Money would be lent to him to make the revolution, and to President A to suppress it. For a time the loans would be so controlled as to keep the rival fighting forces roughly equal. Then, when it appeared that no more could be squeezed out of the country, one of the combatants would be offered far more liberal loans than his rival on the condition that, when successful, he made himself responsible for his rival's debt as well as his own. The Church would be either pillaged or reinstated according to whether it had been found the more convenient to make the liberals or the conservatives win . . . . It [this formula] was used by Woodrow Wilson to establish in power the anti-clerical régime of Madero in Mexico and to depose President Sam from the Presidency of Haiti."

of Boards for Planned Economy and Orderly Marketing are employed, as well as systematic destruction, to diminish and check production. Distribution, already terribly ineffectual, of course, suffers proportionately. The tariffs, quotas and Boards are very effective in reducing production and hampering distribution, but destruction is more spectacular, so it attracts more attention. "In July, 1933, in Liverpool," writes Mr. Jeffrey Mark in *The Modern Idolatry*, "thousands of cases of oranges were dumped into the sea, as it would have been a 'loss to land them.' Up to April 30th, 1932, 5,600,722 bags of coffee had been purchased for destruction by the National Coffee Council of Brazil. Some eight months later, the National Coffee Council announced plans ... for the stabilization of coffee prices, including the destruction of 12,000,000 bags in the next twelve months and the placing of an additional tax of five shillings a bag on coffee exports from the country. The decision to destroy the 12,000,000 bags was reported as unanimous by the *New York Times* of December 7th, 1932. . . In the middle of July, 1933, Mr. Wallace, the Secretary for Agriculture in the United States, announced the success of the scheme (to take land out of cultivation) by the statement that 10,000,000 acres under cotton had been left to waste, the potential crop being thereby reduced by 3,500,000 bales. The bonuses to farmers for this strange attempt to relieve the lot of a half-starved world involved a sum of approximately $100,000,000.

"At the same time, a long drought, heat, and the ravages of grasshoppers united in causing severe damage to the American wheat crop, so that, according to the *London Daily Mail* for the 28th June, 1933, nature is helping President Roosevelt to restrict production, thereby 'paving the way to world recovery.' The news of this triple disaster from drought, blight and grasshoppers was received with acclamation by farmers, salesmen, press and public in the Chicago Wheat Pit, and it is clear that the universal obsession with regard to money and debt has driven the world mad, when there is more joy over one crop that fails than over ninety-nine bounteous harvests."

Similar information about the same points was given in an article in the *Catholic Herald* (London), which stated that "a regular feature of our capitalist-ridden economy was the destruction of the fruits of the earth as a legitimate method of maintaining price levels at a profitable height. Thus, for this reason, in August, 1933, between England and Spain, 1,500,000 oranges were thrown into the sea deliberately. Even more disgraceful has been the pouring into the river Clyde of gallons of rich milk obtained from Irish cows imported and landed in Glasgow. And, of course, the burning of coffee in Brazil is quite well known, although perhaps it is not generally realized on what a gigantic scale this has been done. Between 1931 and 1936 about 40,000,000 bags have been destroyed... enough to supply the whole world for nearly a year and a half."

This destruction is forced upon producers in the endeavor to raise the price of the remainder of their stocks, so that they may make an attempt to pay back a portion of their loans with interest. But the operation of destruction is itself costly. The government must either procure the sum by taxation or borrow it from the banks and then pay it back—with interest—from taxation. In either case the burden upon the producers and consumers is increased. " So that, either way," writes Mr. Mark, "in order to exercise a compulsory privilege to destroy goods which it has itself produced, which it desperately needs, but which it cannot buy because of an existing intolerable debt burden, the community must add to the debt."

Since there seemed to be no immediate possibility of getting the financiers in control to consider the very foundations of the system which was driving the government of the richest country in the world to pay people not to produce, whilst many were suffering from dire want, one man at least drew the logical conclusion. *The U.S.A. Financial Chronicle* for August 18th, 1934, published the following letter to the Editor:—

> Sir,
>
> A friend of mine in New England has a neighbor who has received a check for $1,000 this year for not raising hogs. So my friend wants to go into the business himself, he not being very prosperous just now. He says, in fact, that the idea of not raising hogs appealed to him very strongly. Of course, he will need a hired man, and that is where I come in . . ..
>
> The friend who gets $1,000, got it for not raising 500 hogs. Now we figure that we might easily not raise 1,500 or 2,000 hogs, so you see that the possible profits are only limited by the number of hogs we do not raise. The other fellow has been raising hogs for forty years and never made more than $400 in any one year. Kind of pathetic, isn't it, to think how he wasted his life raising hogs when he could have made so much more by not raising them?
>
> "I will thank you for any advice you may offer.
>
> "Yours very truly, HAROLD TRURMAN."[3]

---

[3] Quoted in *Professor Skinner Alias Montague Norman*, p. 217.

The writer of the above letter had evidently grasped the absurdity of a financial system by which it is more advantageous to pay men a dole for doing nothing than to pay them wages to produce real wealth.

Though it is an obvious fact that it is the defective functioning of the financial system that hampers the production and mutual exchange of all the goods and services available, yet a number of financial experts, as well as many politicians and industrialists speak of *over-production*, while never mentioning *under-consumption* through lack of purchasing power. The paradoxes of *over-production*, such as, hunger in Great Britain while many thousands of tons of wheat lie unsold in the Dominions and Dominion farmers lack many things, machinery, etc., which could be supplied by the unemployed of Great Britain, ships lying idle meantime for lack of freights, are attributed by them to defective arrangements on the part of farmers and manufacturers, and other purely industrial causes. They certainly cannot attribute these paradoxes to lack of transport facilities, or to insufficient development of the arts of advertising and salesmanship. These are more than ample for the work of distribution. Yet ignoring the question of monetary reform, they accept the proposals of the moneyed interests—restriction of production and rationalization of industry.

A brief quotation from G. K. Chesterton's *Chaucer* will fittingly bring this section to a close. "These gallant men," he wrote, "who stormed the gates of the sunset to set up the golden banners of Spain, were fortunately unaware that they were fixing on a peak in Darien the enigmatic ensign that we call the gold standard."

CHAPTER SIX
THE EFFECTS OF THE GOLD STANDARD SYSTEM ON HUMAN LIFE

The purpose of money, according to Saint Thomas, is to facilitate exchanges in view of the development of the supernatural life of members of Christ. We have seen that the functioning of the gold standard has led not only to something of a deadlock in international trade, but to the destruction of food and the lessening of production. The fundamental reason for this has been stated more than once. It lies in the perversion of order involved in the system. Instead of the right order, according to which the manipulation of money is intended to facilitate production, distribution and exchange, in view of strengthening family life, men are now sacrificed for production, while production and consumption, in their turn, are sacrificed for interest on debt. Instead of being an instrument of economics and politics, money is the end. This fundamental disorder, viz., the domination of money shows itself in human life in a multitude of evil effects. Let us consider the disastrous consequences on farming and bread, omitting the trends in regard to ownership, medical service and patent medicines.[1]

FARMING

The production of primary goods is sacrificed to the production of luxury articles and goods of secondary importance. We have seen that the creation of money with a demand for interest leads to goods being unsold in every trade cycle and that the volume unsold increases with the expansion

---

[1] For these points the reader is referred to my book *The Mystical Body of Christ and the Reorganization of Society*, Chapter XIX.

of debt. Now the rhythm of production of secondary and manufactured goods can be accelerated enormously in the endeavor to accomplish the impossible task of getting out of debt. *But agriculture is dependent on the seasons; its rhythm cannot be accelerated in the same proportion, and the attempt to do something similar by the exploitation of virgin soils is disastrous in its effects on those soils.*

This last point can be disposed of first. For an adequate treatment of it the reader is referred to two outstanding books, *The Laboring Earth*, by C. Alma Baker, C.B.E., and *The Rape of the Earth*, by G. V. Jacks and R. O. White. In the introduction to the former by the Rt. Hon. Lord Addison, we read: "There is no doubt as to the justice of the author's first main contention—that, in the desire to make money out of it quickly mankind has wasted the precious earth wholesale, turned fertile lands into deserts and presented us with wide landscapes of rubbish in place of cultivated fields. We have systematically taken organic matter from the soil and not replaced it." The following passages from pages 25 and 28 of the second book are a striking confirmation of Mr. Baker's thesis: " In Europe the countryside has been desecrated and scarred with ugliness in many places, but the one inviolable condition on which man holds the lease of land from Nature—that soil fertility be preserved—has in the main been respected . . .. In the New World . . . with few exceptions, profit and wealth have been most easily won by exploiting and exhausting the virgin soils. In particular grassland soils required only a superficial cultivation to convert them immediately into almost ideal arable soils, rich in plant food, perfect in tilth, and apparently incapable of further improvement. Or they afforded rich and extensive pastures without having to be touched at all. . . The insatiable demands of the Old World and the progress of agricultural science and machinery offered immense profits and further opportunities for exploitation to the man who cashed his soil fertility for labor-saving and yield-increasing devices . . .. Nineteenth century economy, especially within the British Empire, was based on the mutual exchange of agriculture and industrial produce. That the New World was being robbed of its soil and was being paid in coin that brought no recompense to the land never entered the heads of either partner to a bargain which seemed . . . natural, sensible, and highly satisfactory to all concerned."

It did seem quite natural to all concerned, for it was all part of the system of procuring cheap food, in order to keep the wages of English workers low and enable English industry to pay interest on loans contracted from the banks. The domination of finance caused the development of industry in England at the expense of agriculture with its slower rhythmic movement. Then came the importation of cheap food from the virgin soil of America, which resulted in the ruinous exploitation of the latter and brought English agriculture into stagnation and decay. In *The Two Nations* (p. 118), Christopher Hollis points out that the countries that had borrowed from England could only continue to pay even the interest on their debts on condition of exporting something to England. If they did not send something "it would not be possible to raise the new loans with which to pay the interest on the old loans." They could only export food and that food could only find a market in England "on one of two conditions. Only, if either the wages of the poor were raised so that they could buy more than the subsistence quantity of food, or if English domestic agriculture was sabotaged, so as to create a gap which the foreign food could fill. According to the canons of the system, the former alternative, that of raising wages, was inadmissible. Therefore it was necessary to adopt the second and to destroy English agriculture. Hence the necessity for repealing the Corn Laws." Later, on p. 147, he adds that, "owing to the Crimean War and the American Civil War there had been artificial obstacles to prevent the development of a large foreign supply of corn. As late as 1874 there were still 3,821,655 acres under wheat in comparison with about 4,000,000 before Repeal."

"English Farming," writes Commander Herbert Shove, D.S.O., in *The Fairy Ring of Commerce*, "held its own, in a rapidly growing market, for a generation after the repeal of the Corn Laws, but fell again in the eighties, when the exploitation of virgin soil brought it up against a system of living on capital in its own domain, whose products were brought into competition with the homegrown ones through the usurious aid of coal, both in transporting them and cheapening the goods exported to pay for them. The building of the American transcontinental trunk railways marked the final conquest of the English plough by the steam engine."

The same writer points out another revolution which had been going on before that in English farming, under the rule of finance. It was the process of increasing rent by the conversion of tillage land to sheep walks and cattle ranches. The same process was going on in Ireland under the same influences from 1830 to 1880, with an added source of bitterness in the fact that the landlords were aliens in religion and nationality, and the tenants were the dispossessed owners of the soil. Grazing paid better, so human beings gave place to cattle.[2] With the relentless grinding of the

---

[2] Goldsmith's *Deserted Village* depicts in beautiful language some of the consequences of this transformation.

In his *Life of Goldsmith* Macaulay says that *The Deserted Village* is composed of incongruous elements. "The village in its happy days," he writes, "is a true English village. The village in its decay is an Irish village." While

money machine, there came a time when it did not 'pay' to keep up the big houses. It was inevitable.

Let us now take some quotations from unquestioned authorities dealing explicitly with the effect of the domination of finance on agriculture with its seasonal rhythm. "The fundamental processes of farming," writes Sir John Russell in *English Farming*, "are governed by nature's laws and not by our own: seed times and harvest, the period needed to produce an animal, the age at which a cow can begin to give milk—these and many other things which set the pace of farming operations are out of our control. The unit of time is not the day or the week, but the year;

---

not wishing to deny the activity of Goldsmith's imagination, I think that Macaulay, being a Whig, has not taken full account of the English Enclosure Acts, of which, according to the note in the Clarendon Press edition of *The Deserted Village*, there were 700 between 1760 and 1774. "Over three million acres," the note adds, " were thus appropriated (by the landlords) in the eighteenth century in England and in Goldsmith's boyhood a General Napier had enclosed a large tract of land near Lissoy (Ireland) ejecting the cottagers in order to improve his estate." In *The Fairy Ring of Commerce* (p. 114), Commander H. Shove gives the accounts of an English parish about 1746, before enclosure, and about 1786, after enclosure. "The landlord," we read, "obtained £663 more rent. Four farmers at least doubled if not trebled their incomes, and if seventy-eight households were driven off into penury out of this one parish, it was nobody's business and nobody cared."

Other writers, too, may be quoted about the enclosures in England. In *A Shorter History of England* (p. 508), H. Belloc writes: "In the fifty years before the accession of George III (1760) 300,000 acres had been enclosed in the next lifetime seven millions—one-third of the useful land—were taken from the people and went to swell the new capitalist power."

"Under Queen Anne," writes Dr. M. Hashach in *A History of the English Agricultural Laborer* (p. 57), "only two Enclosure Acts were passed under George I, sixteen under George II, as many as 226, making altogether 244 in fifty years. But under George III there were 3,554: and by the end of his reign 5,686,400 acres had been enclosed . . ..Though the Clarendon Press edition of *The Deserted Village* says that Goldsmith had Lissoy in his mind, the above testimonies prove that there is no lack of justification for Goldsmith's lines:

"A time there was, ere England's griefs began,

When every rood of ground maintain'd its man,"

sometimes indeed it is longer, and covers the whole period of the rotation. Farming, therefore, cannot be changed rapidly, and a system once adopted can be altered only slowly; this has often caused farmers to be wrongly regarded as very conservative and unwilling to change their so-called old-fashioned ways.

During three-quarters of the nineteenth century this (famous four-course or Norfolk) rotation proved admirably suited to British conditions, and it was developed to a high standard of technical efficiency.

But from about 1880 onwards the opening up of the North American prairies led to the production of quantities of wheat which was sold here at prices far below those at which our farmers could produce it. Public opinion was entirely against the imposition of any tariff on food, and farmers both on the prairies and at home were left to solve the problem as best they could. The prairie farmers suffered and had to accept a very low standard of living and to adopt methods which led ultimately to terrible destruction of the soil. The home farmers suffered equally; many went under, and there was great distress in the countryside."

"Erosion," writes Lord Northbourne in *Look to the Land,* is nearly all man's work. Some of it can be attributed to mere foolishness. But most of it is due to greed combined with the existence of the possibility of getting rich quickly by exhausting the land and underselling competitors. But the actual tillers of the soil who have got rich are few. What then has been the inducement to so many to despoil the land on which they depend for a living, and to despoil it within the last century or so to a hitherto unheard-of extent? What has been the stimulus to the rapid extension of exhaustive farming all over the world?

"The stimulus has been a great development of the said possibilities of getting rich quickly, a development partly dependent on the evolution of new and powerful machines, and partly on a roughly simultaneous worldwide extension of a peculiar economic system, which has led to a vast accumulation of financial debt. Such debt, both internal and international, has grown to a point at which repayment is generally out of the question, and the payment of interest alone has become severely oppressive. The only way by which one can pay this interest is by producing or manufacturing and selling something with a view to making a money profit out of which to pay it. So purely financial considerations have everywhere acquired dominance over all others... International debt and soil erosion are twin brother and sister, inseparables . . .. Rationalization implies in the end merely an increase of speed. Its object is that the same number of men should produce more in a given time. In applying it we forget that life is a rhythmical process. The 'music of the spheres' is no mere poetic phrase.

It is reflected in the life processes of all creatures and of their associations, and not only so in such obvious physical phenomena as the seasons, the tides, the alternations of night and day, the beating of the heart, or the finer vibrations studied by physicists. The harmonious rhythms of life are thrown into discord by the inexorable urge to speed and ever more speed which is the inevitable accompaniment of a way of life dominated by the mathematical fiction which we know as money . . .. There is another complication. It is the fact that our economic and financial system has an inherent instability. For hundreds of years farm prices have fluctuated wildly. Short booms have been followed by long slumps. . . Instability of prices, when it goes beyond a certain point, takes away whatever chance the farmer might have of coping with the competition with which he is faced. For the farmer's main job is the steady building up of the fertility of the soil, a job quite incompatible with constant changes of policy, forced upon him by changes in the price situation.

"Under present conditions the only thing that pays is quick profit-making while the going is good. By ignorant or unscrupulous exploitation and exhaustion of fertility vast profits have been made (by financiers rather than farmers) in the name of cheap food. The pace is forced for the sound farmer wherever he lives. The time factor becomes ever more and more important, as everyone has to snatch at the chances of the moment to catch up with the accumulation of debt, and achieve a quick turnover to minimize overhead costs per unit of production. If what has been said about the state of farming in the world is true, there is no need to dwell at length on the importance to mankind of a relaxation of the inexorable urge to speed under which both man and the land on which he lives are exhausted. As is usual nowadays, it will be left for future generations to pay for our mistakes, but they may not have the wherewithal. Money alone is notoriously useless in a desert."[3]

"In country after country," writes the Earl of Portsmouth in his fine book, *Alternative to Death*, " the farmer's indebtedness is greater than his capital assets . . .. Thus in Australia, for instance, the average debt of each farmer is more than the capital value of his entire assets in land and stock. The farmer must therefore go bankrupt or continue to pay interest with the produce of his land on a capital sum greater than the value of his holding. To do that he is forced either to over graze his land in order to sell

---

[3] *Look to the Land* is published by Dent and Sons. It is a very remarkable study of the disastrous effects of the monetary system on farming, food etc.

more sheep and wool, or to grow wheat, which exhausts his land, when he should be growing fertility crops such as clover.

The result of this is threefold. First, his own land becomes exhausted and each further step he takes towards repayment of his debt or interest makes the exhaustion greater. Second, by exhausting his own land he is altering the climate, creating drought and erosion, so that if his neighbors are in a like condition as himself, the desert steps in. Third, as if to make quite sure that there is no hope of averting the victory of the desert, he is forced to overcrowd the export market by selling the produce, which is really the capital of his soil, in competition with his neighbors who are likewise impoverished, Thus prices fall and the farmer cannot purchase the produce of industry which then works at half time and half employment. The same type of example could be written of any part of the world except places like the Hunza Valley, where men live with and by the soil, returning everything to it, and know no debt. In other words, it applies practically to the whole of the so-called civilized world where the present machinery for finance and distribution exists . . ..

Although civilization rests on the soil, civilization as we know it is complicated. For the lubrication of its machinery it requires a steady and constant flow of money as the medium of exchange. Therefore, unless there is proper functioning of money, it will be impossible for modern civilization to continue without the parts seizing. This has in fact happened. The first and greatest victim is the soil."[4]

The exhaustion of the soil has deleterious effects on the crops grown thereon, which in their turn lead to ill-health and inability to resist disease in the animals and human beings that feed on them. "The flooding of the English market with cheap food, grown anywhere and anyhow," writes Sir Albert Howard in *An Agricultural Testament,* "forced farmers of this country (England) to throw to the winds the old and well-tried principles of mixed farming, and to save themselves from bankruptcy by reducing the cost of production. But this temporary salvation was paid for by loss of fertility. Mother earth has recorded her disapproval by the steady growth of disease in crops, animals and mankind. The spraying machine was called in to protect the plant; vaccines and serums the animals; in the last resort the afflicted livestock are slaughtered and burnt. This policy is failing before our eyes . . ..The population, fed on improperly grown food, has to be bolstered up by an expensive system of patent medicines, panel doctors, dispensaries, hospitals, and convalescent homes. A C3 population is being

---

[4] *Alternative to Death* is published by Faber and Faber, Ltd.

created . . ... The prophet is always at the mercy of events; nevertheless, I venture to conclude this book with the forecast that at least half the illnesses of mankind will disappear once our food supplies are raised from fertile soil and consumed in a fresh condition."[5]

One more quotation concerning the disastrous effects of soil exhaustion will be given, because of the great authority of the writer. Brig. Gen. Sir Robert McCarrison, Director of Nutrition Research in India, writes "If they (foodstuffs) be produced on impoverished soils, their quality will be poor and the health of those who eat them, man and his domestic animals, will suffer accordingly."[6]

The situation in the world in general may be well summed up in the words of Edmund Blunden in *Return to Husbandry*: "In all continents," we read, "the desert is advancing, smothering the fertile plains and valleys with drifting sands . . ... Civilization has brought us to a pass of mechanized savagery which nothing will cure perhaps except famine and disease. And it is famine and disease which threaten the future which our young people will call their time."[7]

Perhaps what has been written in this section may help people to understand in some degree why farmers, the producers of primary necessities, are everywhere complaining, and why re-forestation in Ireland is not popular financially. *The slower rhythm of agriculture and forestry, so favorable to normal human life, is not beloved of those whose chief preoccupation is interest on debt.* It is to be hoped that, having discovered why, people will strive to do all they can to remedy the state of affairs, instead of treating the complaints of the farming community as a matter for jesting.

BREAD

We shall begin by quoting a few extracts from *Bread in Peace and in War*, a splendid pamphlet published in October, 1940, by the Food Education Society of England. In this excellent work, the facts of the case are outlined as follows "It has been well known for years that civilized diet is deficient in both vitamins and mineral salts. For centuries two of the most important foods of the world have been wheat and rice. Before 1850 these

---

[5] *An Agricultural Testament* is published by the Oxford University Press.
[6] Quoted by K. E. Barlow in *The Discipline of Peace* (Faber and Faber), P. 127.
[7] *Return to Husbandry* is published by J. M. Dent and Sons, Ltd.

grains were pounded by hand or coarsely stone-ground, and little of the bran was lost, while the valuable vitamin B was retained. The introduction of steel rolls for milling enabled the miller to produce finer flour while the bran and so on were sieved off. These sievings contain the germ of the wheat (or rice) and incidentally the vitamin B and the mineral salts. The flour from the modern treatment is whiter, and the public, mistakenly thinking that whiteness means purity and goodness, demands the whitest possible flour. To obtain this, the modern miller bleaches his flour with chemicals. The result of these operations is to produce a devitalized white powder, which we make into bread, but it is no longer the 'staff of life.' The sievings, which contain the most valuable part of the wheat, are made into foodstuffs for poultry or other livestock.

Very powerful commercial interests, including a whole group of advertised cereal goods, drugs, preparations, etc., have been built up upon the circumstances that the milling trade has been ready and able to supply the raw materials of these traders in the form of the so-called 'offal' of flour, which 'offal' was, previous to 1880 (introduction of roller-milling), included in the daily food of the people and is now extracted from it . . .. The attention of the Minister of Food is called to a legal anomaly, now much discussed, and likely to excite feeling when it is more generally appreciated, viz., the dairyman or milk supplier who extracts cream from his milk (beyond a certain percentage) is visited with the most severe penalties; the miller who extracts the equivalent of cream from his flour goes scot-free."

A few passages from another excellent pamphlet, *Our Daily Bread*, by Prof. Joseph Reilly of University College, Cork, may be quoted in confirmation of what we have just said. "The trend of development in the treatment of cereals for human use is not in line with progress in the science of nutrition, but rather in the opposite direction. This applies especially to wheat as used by man in the form of the white loaf. The aim for a long time was to provide a product pleasant in appearance, irrespective of the loss of the finer nutritive constituents. The actual nature of the loaf has changed within the last three or four decades.

"I would like to emphasize this fact that the public should not confuse the present high extraction flour (even 95% extraction) with whole-meal flour. What I mean by whole-meal flour is whole grain, stone-milled flour containing the germ of the wheat as well as all the other constituents of the wheat berry. . Even the roller-milled flour is often bleached still whiter by irritants or oxidized by so-called chemical improvers. Chemicals such as nitrosylchloride, chlorine, nitric acid, benzoyl peroxide or certain persulphates are also used . . .. Nitrogen tri-chloride has largely displaced other chemicals in the bleaching of flour. About 90% of the flour mills in North America and 85% of the flour mills in England employ this reagent. An extremely white product results. It is claimed that this treatment, even though it increases cost, alters the gluten and gives the baker a more stable and stiffer dough so that on the treatment with yeast a 'better' loaf results which will absorb more water—hence more loaves per sack of flour." [8]

In spite of these undeniable facts, the struggle to secure good bread for the people, especially for the poor, will be exceedingly difficult. The big mills with their large output 'pay' better than the other type, which turned out better flour. The pamphlet, *Bread in Peace and War*, continues: "Today (in regard to this struggle) we have to contend with a more powerful opposition (than in 1917) because the flour milling industry is in the hands of so few firms. This is a great danger. In 1930 when Mr. Hurst wrote his brochure on The Bread of Britain, the Co-operative Wholesale Society milled 22% of the flour, Ranks 20%, Spillers 20%, and independent firms 32%. Hurst said that it would not be long before 80% was controlled. Now 90% is controlled by the three. Powerful interests such as these are never going to release their hold so long as they can persuade the public that white flour is the right stuff . . .. What are the circumstances which explain the resistance to the provision of a whole-meal bread? May they not be found in the fact that the entire industry of flour milling in this country is now for practical purposes concentrated in one gigantic combination which approximates to the position of a single trust, inasmuch as two private and interrelated firms, with the Co-operative Wholesale Society as their sole rival, control the whole production of flour? Any departure from existing practice must mean a serious disturbance of invested capital amounting at this time probably to something like 20 million sterling, and the loss to the companies concerned of the highly profitable byproducts of milling white flour . . .. Mr. John Burns, President, Local Government Board, announced that a bill was in preparation to secure the purity of flour and to render illegal the use of phosphates and bleaching, July 23, 1912. The same Minister stated that a bill dealing with the whole question of the purity of food, including flour was in preparation, March 26, 1913. Neither measure, however, saw the light.

"In a democracy," writes Mr. Kenny Williamson in the *Monthly Bulletin* of the Economic Reform Club, July, 1941, "free speech is permitted. You can say what you think, within limits, the limits imposed by the 'money power'. I have done a little broadcasting; but could I say what I thought, what I believed? Of course not. In 1938 I wrote a script

---

[8] *Our Daily Bread* is published by The Forum Press, Cork.

that experiments at Cambridge, upon rats fed exclusively on white bread, had resulted in the rats dying of various diseases (all due to malnutrition) within three months. I was not allowed to say this, however. Nor was I permitted to extol the virtues of whole-meal bread. I was not allowed to explode the old lie that British wheat was unfit for making into whole-meal flour. The 'money power' had mills at the ports and its machinery was designed for skimming the nutritious golden skin of the harder foreign wheat-berry, in order to produce snow white flour, and also to supply the feeding stuffs trade with 'offals' as the skins or rinds are called. If everyone hearing my talk, made sudden demand for wheat-meal bread, millions of pounds worth of machinery would have to be scrapped. Sixteen million people might be permanently under-nourished but sixteen million pounds must not be lost! . . .. Nothing likely to injure the 'money power' was permitted... Be a good boy and prophesy unto them smooth things, or else you won't be able to give any more talks over the air of the BBC. Sixteen millions permanently under-nourished? We are afraid it has nothing to do with us. Privately, of course, we agree with you, but orders are orders.

"It was the same in newspaper articles: nothing must be printed which might cause a falling off of advertising revenue. In one group of newspapers the jolly Millers spent over forty thousand pounds in advertising, so nothing depreciating white flour must appear in the paper. Won't you write another article instead about the otter? Say just what you like. They live in water, don't they, in rivers and swamps? . . ..The 'money power' cares nothing for human life, nothing for the soil that is the mother of human life. How long will men continue to respect the old system which is based on the 'money power'? For the system not only ruins the soil and despoils human life, but periodically it becomes locked in a deadly struggle with its rivals."

Bread is not the only food of which the quality has deteriorated as a result of man's reversal of the natural order. "The farmer's produce is no longer conveyed to the local market," writes Arthur Rogers, "by the most economic form of transport for this purpose, which is still a horse-drawn cart. This has led to a great reduction in the supply of one of the most valuable of natural and living fertilizers, which has been replaced by combine produced dead chemical de-fertilizers. . . .. The under nourishment, which is a justifiable cause for concern, is due to the quality rather than to the quantity of the food eaten by our town dwellers. The most nourishing food is fresh, natural food which has been produced on living soil. Food consumed in our cities is mostly stale, denatured food, produced on chemically deadened and denatured soil. This is the major cause of declining fertility . . .while the denatured condition of the soil is also one of the chief reasons for foot-and-mouth disease . . . .. Milk is robbed of its vitality by pasteurization, which can be undertaken only by the big milk combines and which, if enforced, must tend to squeeze out great numbers of independent producers and retailers. Before wheat is used for breadmaking it's germ is taken out alive. Only now under stress of war conditions, is it put back dead. The extracted wheat germ is sold at about ten times the price of flour. These processes are inspired by big business . . .. Big business influences are the chief cause of the widespread undernourishment.[9] And big business is the interest slave of finance, to use Viscount Lymington's expression when speaking of the farmers of the Middle West.[10]

---

[9] *Our Peace Crisis*, pp. 66, 67 (The Sterling Press, 38, Bedford Street, London, W.C.2). For a corroborative testimony, cf. *Look to the Land*, by Lord Northbourne, pp. 68–74.

[10] Famine in England; p. 94. On the same page, Viscount Lymington sums up the situation in the United States as follows: "There is no democracy, but only three main classes in the western world today: the wage-slave, the interest-slave and the plutocrat."

CHAPTER SEVEN
USURY

In the examination of this question, we must keep well before our minds the text of Pope Leo XIII in the Encyclical Letter, *Rerum Novarum* (1891), where he insists upon the existence of usury in our day, though under a different guise from that of ancient times. After having pointed out that the abolition of the guilds and the free rein given to unbridled competition had opened the way to the subjection of the laboring poor to a small number of wealthy men, he adds: "The evil has been increased by rapacious usury which though more than once condemned by the Church, is, nevertheless, under a different guise, but with like injustice, still practiced by covetous and grasping men." It must be emphasized that the Pope used the present tense to indicate that he is affirming the existence of usury at the time of writing. He then goes on to point out that the evil in question, namely, the growth of a vast propertyless proletariat in subjection to a few rich men, has been still further augmented by the uprise of powerful monopolies controlling enterprises and raw materials. Usury, therefore, according to Pope Leo XIII, not only exists in our times, but it has played an enormous part in depriving the masses of property and concentrating it in the hands of a few. Of course, in regard to this particular point, I am only giving as probable the explanation set out below. As Father McLaughlin, O.S.B., says in an able article, *Usury Sub Judice*, in *The Clergy Review* (January 1935) : "The problem of usury is still undecided and has been for centuries. The Church will not decide it until discussion among theologians has been deep enough and accurate enough to lay bare the dividing line between 'that fruit which is drawn from money by just right and therefore can be kept both in law and in conscience; and that other fruit which is drawn from money wrongly, and therefore must be adjudged to be repaid, both by law and by conscience' (Pope Benedict XIV, Ency. Letter, *Vix Pervenit*)."

Many writers hold with Father Lamarche, O.P., in *La justice et le Prêt á Intérét*, that "modern lending is so constituted that always and everywhere it is accompanied by extrinsic titles justifying interest." Accordingly, they maintain that usury, except in the sense of exorbitant interest, does not exist, because extrinsic titles justifying a certain rate of interest are always present. For these writers, however, money as a fungible thing, has an existence independent of the lender and the borrower. "A fungible thing," writes Father Lewis Watt, S.J., in *The Ethics of Interest*, "is one which perishes in the act of serving its natural purpose . . . . The natural and normal use of a loaf of bread, for instance, is to be eaten . . . .. The loaf is a fungible thing." The money of which these writers speak, therefore, exists prior to being lent. A loan for them is the transfer of a pre-existing claim for goods and services which the lender has acquired. The lender gives up something. But when bankers grant loans, they bring exchange medium into existence—they create money. They are not simply lending exchange medium having an existence independent of them and of the borrowers. "Borrowing," writes Prof. O'Rahilly in *Money* "covers (1) the transfer of pre-existing claims legitimately earned by the holders; (2) the creation of new money claims . . .. The government does not and cannot borrow pre-existing money from the banks: all it can do is to pay them for creating new money." As Professor Soddy insists, the banks do not give up anything at all.

Accordingly, other writers point out that four out of the five extrinsic titles, namely, *lucrum cessans* (gain given up), *damnum emergens* (resulting loss), *periculum sortis* (risk) and *poena conventionalis* (liability to a forfeit,) properly apply only where the lender of money gives up already existing money created independently of him, which by his industry he has succeeded in acquiring. Professor Soddy states this in his usual clear style: "The evils of genuine usury in the Middle Ages," he writes, "through the shortage of the precious metals and the insufficiency of the medium of exchange, cried aloud to heaven for redress. But the genuine usurer did at least give up what he lent and that for which he received interest, whereas the banker does not . . .. It is bad enough to be in the grip of the moneylender who does lend his money, but it is a million times worse to be in the grip of the pretended moneylender who does not lend his own money but creates it to lend and destroys the means of repayment just as fast as the debtors succeed in repaying it." Sir Reginald Rowe implicitly makes the same assertion, namely, that exchange medium is created and cancelled in the manner best calculated to make profit for the creators. " It is the large variations in the rate of interest," he writes, "brought about in the past by the international scramble for gold, which seems to me largely responsible for present day evils, including a world continually at war. Internally they are the machinery of alternate inflations and deflations, an alternation which hits everybody except the dealers in money *who profit on balance either way*. Thereby the trader, whether merchant or manufacturer, is hurt on balance, and all wage earners, a vast majority of the community, suffer excessively."

Of course, Professor Soddy and Sir Reginald Rowe and all the writers on modern money admit that the banks are allowed to make a service charge for the creation of exchange medium and that in this way there is a valid title to a certain percentage for bank loans. This is the equivalent of *Lex civilis* or the title of civil law, of which theologians speak. As the function is a public service it can be conceded that the banks have a right to a reasonable remuneration, but as Professor O'Rahilly points out, the term interest cannot properly be applied to bank charges for the issue of bank money.

Accordingly, a moderate service charge is justified. But are the banks content with this? Sir Reginald Rowe expresses the attitude of mind of the growing body of students of the banking system on this point, when he writes: "New economists are not prepared to admit that banking could not be worked much more cheaply, but even if banking administration cost no less, they think it fatally wrong that the creation and destruction of money should be left to private concerns owned by shareholders. The banks publish balance sheets, but no profit and loss accounts. Their operations are largely kept secret; their balance sheets leave much unrevealed. They can always, through their power in the manufacture of credit, arrange to pay a 15% dividend (which seems to be about the figure which their directorates judge will not alarm the public), or any large dividend within reasonable limits." It is interesting to note that state created money, for example, silver and copper coins, circulates without interest being paid on it, while bank created money enables a dividend of 15%, to be paid on its circulation. Though a moderate rate of interest on the creation of money can be justified as a service charge, yet all Catholic writers agree that an excessive rate of interest is usurious. This, however, can hardly be what Pope Leo XIII meant when he said that usury had come back under another guise, for it is an old form of usury.

It seems fairly obvious that the manner in which usury has come back in modern times under another form is by the arbitrary changes made in the volume of exchange medium by those who are in chief control of the monetary system. The argument must be understood to be exclusively against "the financial leaders who direct its major operations," to use Sir Reginald Rowe's words. The deflation after the Great War (1914–18), which told so hardly on Irish farmers, was certainly not the working out of an inexorable law of nature like a drought in Australia. Money is manipulated by human intelligences and wills responsible for the "scarcity of money" spoken of by Pope Pius XI in the Encyclical Letter, *On the Troubles of Our Time.*

"It is the big financiers, the dealers in big money," writes Sir Reginald Rowe in *The Root of All Evil*, "who control the machine by directing the movements of credit; and this gives them immense power over the rest of us . . .. Those in chief control of money are comparatively few, but the army they command is large, since it contains all those whose livelihood is associated with the movements of money. I think that many of the leaders, if not all, understand the problem perfectly well, but keep it as far as possible from their own consideration as well as from that of others . . .. Of the rank and file (of the monetary army), probably not one in a hundred understands the problem at all. Books are written about it, which they do not read, and it is hardly ever mentioned in the press . . .. I think many of them are beginning to doubt if it (the present system) is satisfactory . . .. The press is hugely capitalized, must pay interest on its capital, and has to finance itself on the large scale which is so dear to the heart of the money power. In the present state of public ignorance no important newspaper dare affront and challenge the 'money power' for fear of the consequences. Our credit makers, the banks, serving in their turn 'big money,' could easily, by a twist of the credit screw, check any such revolt."

Arbitrary changes in the volume of money or exchange medium cause prices to rise and fall. Thus the power to change the volume of the exchange medium is the power to change the terms of every contract involving future money payments. The amount of currency or exchange is increased if the aggregate of loans granted is greater than the aggregate of loans paid back or called in, as happens in periods of credit expansion. The amount of currency is decreased if the aggregate of loans granted is less than the aggregate of loans called in or paid back, as happens in periods of credit contraction. One party to the loan contract, the central bank in control of the issue of credit money, thus retains the power to alter the value of the currency as a measure of things saleable. This is the same as if a man sells a horse to another, and at the same time retains the power to change the animal into a mule or a donkey in a fortnight or whenever it suits him. The yard measure or the pound avoirdupois is not alterable in this way at the will of a buyer or a seller. One of the contracting parties, the central bank, plays the accordion with the exchange medium and can thus double the 5%. There can be no question of extrinsic titles in this case. It is purely and simply usury under another guise, that is, a charge made for the transfer of exchange medium on no other ground than that of the fact of transferring its ownership.

In his recently published work, *Interest and Usury*, the Rev. Bernard Dempsey, S.J., seems to hold this.[1] He writes: "Deflation did not present itself to them (the Scholastics) as an acute problem. . . If the loans and created funds were all in the hands of one man, the Scholastics would not approve of that one man calling all the loans simultaneously, inducing distress selling and an avalanche of pseudo-costs with resultant lower values, and then buying in the assets. That, too, would be gain from a loan and to make one's own price by calling a loan would be no less reprehensible than charging a higher price for a good which the seller financed by a loan involving no emergent loss. Though the Schoolmen were not confronted with the problem, we may well believe that they would have condemned such a practice as heartily as they would condemn the depreciation of money by sending pseudo-income to market."

This is the point made by Mr. Arthur Kitson in *A Fraudulent Standard*, published in 1917, where he speaks of the plans of the great banking and financial companies that had invested large sums in war loans, by a mere stroke of the pen, to double the weight of the war debt. They were planning to do this, he said, by returning to the gold standard and thus altering the value of the pounds in which the debt had been contracted. "Similarly," he adds, "although the nominal rate of interest is 5% by this method of tampering with the value of the pound, these investors will actually receive 10% of their original investment.[2] The return to the gold standard took place in 1925 and the taxpayers had to sell two sheep instead of one, in order to pay the interest, though the nominal figures of the debt and of the interest were not changed. This certainly seems to be usurious, and it accompanies all the 'booms' and 'slumps' or inflations and deflations that are part of the normal functioning of the gold standard. The consequences of declining prices are business failures, unemployment and wholesale foreclosures with inevitable increasing financial control. 'Inflation,' as Mr. Jeffrey Mark expresses it in *The Modern Idolatry*, "is the web of the financial spider, and deflation the mastication of the human fly."

---

[1] *Interest and Usury* is published by the American Council on Public Affairs, Washington.

[2] "In his 1924 address, referring to the intended return to the gold standard, Mr. McKenna stated that the national debt 'stands today at £7,700 millions, mostly borrowed when money was worth very much less than before the war. With prices back to their former level, the true burden of the debt will be more than doubled. The creditor will receive a huge premium at the expense of the debtor. "(Article on the Bank of England in *The Weekly Review*, Sept. 26th, 1940).

In order not to be unfair to those who control the monetary system, I should like to quote a passage from the Earl of Portsmouth's splendid book, *Alternative to Death*. The noble writer distinguishes between the controllers and the system as follows: "Probably no country in the world has such able or upright controllers of its banking system as we have. One of the very reasons why the devil has never been sufficiently visible to provoke revolt is the fact that some of the most honest of men have devoted their lives in all sincerity to the elaboration of this nevertheless dishonest system. Because they have rarely been over-greedy, they have worked the system sufficiently well to mask our decline to the servile state by imperceptible stages.

The great joint stock banks have a probity over detail which is almost medieval in its honesty. But while they continue to work such a system, based upon power without responsibility and profit without production, misery and degradation have walked at the head of the procession of modern progress."[3]

THE ENGLISH MONETARY SYSTEM AND IRELAND

Under the present monetary system, we in Ireland are suffering from the same evils as the people of England, but in an accentuated fashion. We have the same monetary system, but, if I may use a popular expression, we are the tail of the dog. If the head and body of the dog are getting badly hit and are growling, the tail is getting a still worse deal and has far more reason to complain. "We must not be mislead by current phraseology," writes Professor O'Rahilly in *Money* (p. 394), "into thinking that we have at present a separate currency which happens to be kept at parity with British currency. What we have is not parity but identity subject to separate book entry." This identity was disastrous for our farmers, when the Bank of England, as we have seen, entered upon its deflationary process after the Great War. The nominal 5% on their bank loans became in reality 10% owing to the decrease in the quantity of exchange medium, so they had to sell two animals instead of one, in order to pay their interest. The consequences during the present war (1939–?), are also very sad. Owing to

---

[3] Christopher Hollis is more cynical. "The individual gentleman," he writes, "would ... be unwilling to do anything that would let down the school, or the regiment, or what not. But, if you could trick the whole school into connivance at injustice, then on the gentleman's code, it would become disloyalty to question the conduct of the school. So Shylock exchanged the Jewish gaberdine for the Old School Tie and was elected with acclamation to the governing body" (*The Two Nations*, p. 50).

the fact that our Currency Commission or central bank may and must issue currency for internal purposes only if and when sterling is surrendered to them," those who have a bullock or other animal to sell can secure English money and so obtain Irish exchange medium, but those who have only their labor to sell must go to England, where new English exchange medium is issued, in order to obtain it. Now it would take a long time to imbue most Irish men and women with Communistic ideas in Irish surroundings, but in non-Catholic surroundings, with a paper like *Irish Freedom* giving them the Communistic viewpoint on Irish affairs and world events, the situation is different. The morally inevitable consequences of the migration and return fit in well with the plans of the organized anti-supernatural forces in the world for the attack on the supernatural life of our country. I have dealt with this last matter briefly in my pamphlet, *The Workingmen's Guilds of the Middle Ages*. Professor O'Rahilly has frequently pointed out in *The Standard* that our central bank is powerless to control our price level.[4]

In the May (1944) issue of *Irish Freedom* the confiscation of Church property and the denial of the right of acquiring property by inheritance were lauded as "sound, democratic principles." We need to bear in mind that revolutions against the Catholic church and the Mass are not spontaneous uprisings of the people. They are movements prepared a long time in advance by the forces organized against our Divine Lord and the supernatural life of grace.[5] The art of revolution is that by which a small but well organized minority compels an unwilling but unorganized majority to submit to the overthrow of the state. The method is the same today as it was in 1789–1793, namely, the creation of a revolutionary atmosphere by the exploitation of existing grievances.[6] There is a grievance ready to hand in our country in the failure of our successive native governments to deal with unemployment and emigration. Every effort will be made to canalize the discontent of the poor with this failure into revolt against religion and private property. It will be proclaimed loudly that only by a Communist revolution can the full fruits of the Irish Rising of 1916 be reaped. It will be insisted that unemployment and emigration prove that the 'masses' who made possible the success of the Rising have been betrayed. The functioning of the monetary system in Ireland has certainly

---

[4] Professor O'Rahilly in *The Standard*, 9th Oct., 1942.

[5] Cf. *The Kingship of Christ and Organized Naturalism, The Mystical Body of Christ and the Reorganization of Society* and *The Mystical Body of Christ in the Modern World*.

[6] Cf. *The Mystical Body of Christ and the Reorganization of Society*, chapter 5.

contributed towards the growth of the conditions Communists desire to see, in view of their anti-supernatural designs.

In *The Two Nations* (p. 200), when speaking of the American War of Independence, Christopher Hollis makes the remark that, after a successful revolution, there is usually a second struggle to decide whether the independence is to be true independence or "whether the financial system will re-establish over the new government the same control it had exercised over the old." We in Ireland must bear in mind that the worldwide struggle to bring those skilled in the manipulation of exchange medium into the place in states to which the hierarchical position of their art entitles them is part of the wider struggle for the integral return to the Divine Plan for Order in the world.

CHAPTER EIGHT
OUTLINE OF PRINCIPLES OF MONETARY REFORM

In an excellent pamphlet, entitled *The Arch-Enemy of Economic Freedom*,[1] Professor Soddy, one of the signatories to the Letter quoted in chapter 1, deals succinctly with the evils of the present monetary system and explains the points put before His Grace, the Apostolic Delegate to Great Britain, and the non-Catholic dignitaries. The outline of reform set forth in this pamphlet may be summed up in the author's own words in another of his books: "As regards transition stages, fix a price index on the cost of the more important expenses of an average middle class householder, require the banks always to keep pound for pound of national money against their current accounts drawable by check, set up a national advisory statistical bureau on an independent scientific basis [to see to the stability of the price level], and reconstitute the mint for the issue of all money. Avoid as the plague schemes for nationalizing banks. The object is to stop private minting and nationalize money itself."[2] These points will be amplified in the following paragraphs.[3]

NATIONAL MONETARY REFORM

(a)—Abandonment of the Domestic Gold Standard
From what we have seen of the functioning of the domestic gold standard, it will be evident that it is opposed to the common good to have the volume of exchange medium in a country proportioned, not to the

---

[1] The pamphlet can be obtained from the author at Knapp, Enstone, Oxon., England. Is. 1 1/2d, post free. [Ed. note 2010 – this is no longer available from the author]

[2] *The Role of Money*, p. 211.

[3] These paragraphs form a portion of Chapter XXI of *The Mystical Body of Christ and the Reorganization of Society.*

actualization of the country's potential productivity, but to the amount of gold that may happen to be in the country. "The aura of security that still hangs about gold," writes Mr. Geoffrey Crowther, "is, in fact, the only remaining sound or semi-sound argument left for the domestic gold standard. In France and America there would probably be anxious distrust in the national currencies, if they were not known to be 'backed by gold.' In England we already have a more rational approach. As has already been pointed out, the gold backing of the Bank of England's notes has been reduced virtually to nothing, and the whole gold reserve has been concentrated in the Exchange Equalization Account, where it is available for export, but not as currency backing. The ordinary man is probably not yet aware that this has happened, but after a few years it will be accepted by the public that money does not need either to be gold or to be backed by gold in order to be good money When that time comes the domestic gold standard will have died a natural death without its demise having done anybody any harm.[4] About this first point of reform there will be no difficulty.

(b)—Issuing of Lawful Exchange Medium by the State

Great evils have resulted from the functioning of the gold standard and the control of the exchange medium of countries by private individuals. To remedy these evils in a manner fully in accordance with the political and economic principles of Saint Thomas, three points must be remembered. The first point of reform is that the *creation* or issuing of exchange medium must be taken out of private hands.[5] The issuing of claims to goods and services valid and acceptable to all the citizens of a country is by right the prerogative of the authority exercising jurisdiction over the whole country. This is clearly seen by the fact that additional credit money issued or loaned into existence, if it does not happen to coincide with a proportional increase of goods for sale, " will raise prices and make the value of everybody's money in the country worth less in goods, so repudiating part of the nation's debt in goods and services to the owners of money."[6] To put

---

[4] *An Outline of Money*, p. 333.

[5] The three points, which will be developed under (b), (c), and (d), are taken from *Money Creators* (Chapters XII and XVII), by Miss G. M. Coogan. In the foreword to this book, Mr. Robert L. Owen says that "it contains scientific truths—not quackery." Mr. Owen is a former Chairman of the Banking and Currency Committee of the United States Senate.

[6] *The Role of Money*, by Professor Soddy (p. 91). The private creators of exchange medium are not concerned about the alterations of the

this another way, whoever originates the exchange medium must, by the very nature of money or exchange medium, obtain something for nothing, that is, he must obtain the original purchasing power throughout the state, at a trifling cost. Again, whoever has the power to issue the exchange medium controls the volume of it. Arbitrary changes in the volume of money cause prices to rise or to fall. Whoever originates and controls the volume of money thus controls every single economic operation. If a private group exercises the power to originate the exchange medium and then manipulates the volume of it, that group becomes a power greater than the government itself. It becomes a super-government, paralyzing the efforts of the lawful government for the common good. It is perfectly idle to talk about a democracy or a republic, when the sovereign power is really being exercised by an individual super-group.[7] In his excellent book, *Economic Tribulation*, Mr. V. C. Vickers points out this truth and its consequences. "Through our own base carelessness and ignorance," he writes, "we have permitted the money industry, by the very virtue of its business, gradually to attain a political and economic influence so wide and powerful that it has actually undermined the authority of the state and usurped the power of democratic government . . .. This national and mainly international dictatorship of money, which plays off one country against another, and which, through the ownership of a large portion of the press, converts the advertisement of its own private opinion into the semblance of general public opinion, cannot for much longer be permitted to render Democratic government a mere nickname . . ..The finance industry, the exchange bankers and the Stock Exchange grow rich upon the ups and downs of trade, and are largely dependent on variations and changes of the price level of commodities. But productive industry grows

---

price-level. Their preoccupation is with interest on money. " Professor Soddy is very insistent that . . . the banks by the issue of new money to themselves or their borrowers actually enforce a direct levy in kind on the wealth-on-sale of the community (i.e. on all there is for sale). . . Anyone can see that this is the case when a counterfeit note is put in circulation, but the forced levy on the wealth-on-sale is just the same whoever creates the new money" (*The Root of All Evil*, by Sir Reginald Rowe, p. 52).

[7] "We have always maintained that the foreign policy of this country where it came into touch with exceptional expenditure upon international action—notably in connection with English armament depended upon the decision . . .of the Bank of England supported by their financial allies beyond the Atlantic . . .. They were certainly opposed to an adequate army." (*The Weekly Review*, Oct. 17th, 1940).

rich upon stable markets, a constant price level, and the absence of violent economic fluctuations.

Under such general conditions, the Communist is naturally content to bide his time for he observes that the trend of affairs is slowly converging towards the very conditions he most desires to see—a growing discontent with finance and the money system, an increasing weariness of the present form of party government, and an increasing poverty and loss of influence among those who have so recently been the mainstay and backbone of their country."[8]

As nations have to struggle to maintain their national sovereignty against the international manipulators of money, the sovereign authority in the nation must take over the creation of the entire medium of exchange, consisting of the lawful physical or tangible money of the country. Private individuals engaged in finance cannot be entrusted with the struggle to safeguard national sovereignty against "the deadly and detestable international imperialism of money," to use the words of Pope Pius XI.[9] This is especially important since bankers in every country have already succumbed to its rule and are accustomed to look upon the trends favored by it as indicative of the true line of progress for the world. They have hitherto conspicuously failed to practice the virtue of general or legal justice.

Accordingly, the entire medium of exchange, *consisting of the lawful money of each country,* should be paid into use by the sovereign power in the country. No private promises-to-pay should be allowed to circulate as legal tender but should be subjected to the penalties applying to counterfeit money. The money created and paid into use by the sovereign power should be non-interest bearing at the source and non-cancelable, except by recalling it through taxation. It should not be brought into existence as a loan. The whole amount of new money issued should be paid into circulation to defray legitimate government expenses or to pay off existing government debt. The people, as a whole, would thus share the benefits and advantages involved in a change in the volume of money in existence in a nation. "By placing this first buying power in the hands of the government,

---

[8] *Economic Tribulation* is published by John Lane, The Bodley Head, London.

[9] The Pope's words in the Encyclical Letter, *Quadragesimo Anno,* are: "*funestus et exsecrandus rei nummariae 'internationalismus' seu 'imperialismus internationalis' cui, ubi bene, ibi patria est.*" This 'International Imperialism', will tend to eliminate all that is enshrined in the Catholic concept of '*patria*'. This end coincides with that of Marx's dictum: "Workmen have no country."

the benefits fall to all the people, for by whatever amount the new money is issued, tax collections may be correspondingly reduced. This statement can be twisted into the thought that taxes can be abolished by merely issuing money *ad infinitum*. This is fallacious, for new money should be paid into use (circulation) only as the total stock of consumer goods—the things the people have produced and need in civilization—has been increased by expanded production.[10] Besides, it seems opposed to the dignity of human personality that the issuing of exchange medium necessary for the common good should place some in the position of inferiority, as happens when money is loaned into existence. As we shall presently see, the sovereign power in the state should not engage in *lending* money.

(c)—Lending of Lawful Exchange Medium by Banking Guild

The creation of exchange medium, then, should be withdrawn from private individuals. It should be reserved to the national government, but the lending of money should be completely divorced from money origination. This is the second point of monetary reform. The *lending* of the lawful money issued by the governmental monetary authority should not be carried out by the governmental monetary authority, but by privately owned corporations erected into a guild and functioning under a guild charter. Let us take these two proposals in turn.

"The most dangerous thing that could be done would be to place the merchandising of money in the hands of the national government. Such a step would give the internationalists their final weapon to destroy the property and personal rights of loyal citizens."[11] Government in the lending business is the essence of Socialism or Communism. For a government to create money as loans is even more vicious than for private banks to create money as loans; for, in the case of private banks, arbitrary discrimination is not the primary motive in denying loans. No private business can long endure if the government engages in the lending of money even money created by itself, or determines what businesses may acquire savings from the people in return for part ownership. This seems to be a grave defect in the German banking system, even though the fallacy of making the volume of exchange medium of a country depend on the amount of gold under the control of the government has been decisively shown up in that country. It is quite true that the volume of exchange medium ought to be

---

[10] *Money Creators*, by Miss G. M. Coogan, p. 333.

[11] op. cit., p. 334.

proportioned to the development of a country's productive capacity, not to the amount of gold in its central bank. But the German financial system as a whole, in conjunction with the race-theory, will tend to disregard human personality. The Reichsbank creates bank credit as *loans* to the German government, and the German government allows this new bank credit to reach the channels of trade by granting *loans* of it to whatever businesses it arbitrarily chooses. This means that the German government is *determining* what businesses may, or may not, borrow. Such acts of a government allow it to *aid* the businesses it chooses via *granting loans*, and destroy those it chooses by *denial of loans*. This method destroys the individual person's right to the disposal of his own earnings and the inalienable right of the human person to own, use and control honestly acquired private property. As has already been remarked, the human being is thus in danger of becoming a mere individual at the mercy of the state. He is not being treated as a person.[12]

With regard to the second proposal, namely, that the lending of money should be carried out by privately owned corporations, "each of the existing banks should be divided into two separate institutions or at least into departments of the original bank. The first set would be *girobanks*,[13] The Americans designate them 'check banks.' All banks carrying deposits subject to check would be required to treat these deposits as trust-funds

---

[12] Miss Coogan wrote as follows in 1937: "If the government controls the lending of money, it can determine who may, or who may not, borrow money and hence can control every single business in the country. Controlling every business means controlling every economic activity control of every economic activity gives power to control also the cultural and spiritual activities of the citizen. Lenin recommended government origination and control of the medium for exchange. Unless the power to originate money is restricted to sovereignty and scientifically exercised, and lending is restricted exclusively to private, independent, state chartered corporations, it is nothing short of childish prattle to talk about preventing the onrush of Socialism, Communism, or whatever name one wants to use to designate an anti-Christian state, in which all but the 'chosen few' are hopeless slaves."

[13] A *girobank* is a bank in which the money (coins or bullion in the early days) remains the property of the customers or members, thus being a *depositum* in the strict sense, the banker being a custodian or bailee. The owners can withdraw the money and the ownership of it can be transferred by written orders. Hence when the claims are circulated from one to another, they are said to make a giro (a circuit or turn) from hand to hand.

of money held for the depositors . . .. A full 100% reserve has the status of a trust fund, the real owners of which are the depositors.[14] Thus bank deposits would once more become real *deposits* entrusted to the banker and withdrawable on demand. No interest would of course be paid on them; on the contrary, the depositors would have to pay the bank for its book-keeping service in arranging for transfers by check . . .. In addition to *girobanks* there would be loan banks, but not so limited in their scope, for lending or investing. How would these new savings banks get money to lend? From their own money (capital), from the money received from customers (savings accounts), from the money repaid on maturing loans . . .. The only new limitation on bank loans would be a wholesome one, namely, that no money could be lent unless there was money to lend. That is, the banks could no longer over-lend by manufacturing money out of thin air so as to cause inflation and a boom . . .. Under the 100% system, banks would make loans just like anybody else, either out of their own savings or out of somebody else's, precisely as the early lending banks did before they were prevented by somebody's 'bright idea' to lend other people's money while still letting those other people think that they had that money to use as money.[15]

(d)—Stability of Price Level

To understand how the stability of the price level is to be obtained, we must consider the method by which it is proposed to issue and lend lawful exchange medium. Sir Reginald Rowe gives an excellent summary of Professor Soddy's proposals[16] for England as follows: "The huge balance of liabilities for cash which the banks have in fact no means of meeting should be met by the nation by an equivalent issue of national money in the form of notes, and there should be no further creation or destruction of money by the banks. A national issue equal to the total of current bank deposits would be needed, say £2,000 million. The state would take over from the banks securities to this amount. Where these were collateral securities against loans, their owners could redeem them by repaying the loans. Where the state became the owner of government securities, having paid for them with national notes, it could cancel these securities. Any other securities could be exchanged by market process for government securities. The conclusion of the whole matter would be that the banks

---

[14] Irving Fisher, *100 % Money*, 2nd Ed. (1936).

[15] op. cit., pp. 17, 92. The quotation from Irving Fisher is taken from *Money*, by Professor O'Rahilly, pp. 350–352.

[16] Contained in *Wealth, Virtual Wealth and Debt.*, pp. 196–199.

would hold money (physical money in the form of notes) to the exact value of their total current account deposits. It would be real money, a great part of which (i.e. all current account balances) they could not lend, but must hold in trust for its individual owners. [Money on time-deposit could be lent in the fashion already explained above under (c)]. The banks could not create money to lend, as now. One obvious result would be that when £2,000 million had been issued in new notes, that amount of national debt would have been cancelled. It should be emphasized that the issue of further new money would not be at the mercy of any government, but in the hands of a statutory independent body, which would work scientifically on data readily obtained. Its economic thermometer would be price level, the maintenance of average price level being its single aim when increasing or decreasing the supply of money.[17]

We can supplement the above succinct statements by quotations from Miss Coogan's *Money Creators* and A. N. Field's *The Truth about New Zealand*. According to the former, a statistical authority, called the U.S.A. Monetary Trustees, appointed by and directly responsible to the legitimate government, should determine the rate at which lawful money should be issued or withdrawn, in order to maintain the price index of the main commodities constant at a level which would permit full employment. "The Monetary Trustees," she writes, "should maintain scientific records of prices—price indices which would reliably indicate at what levels the aggregate of raw commodities and aggregate finished goods are changing hands at any particular time. Once raw material price levels had reached a point wherein the nation's productive arid business activity had absorbed its unemployed, and the price structure was high enough to afford sufficient national income to carry the legitimate private debt structure of the nation, that price level should be maintained. The fluctuations thereafter should be minor, because the flow of money would always be scientifically related to the actual quantity of physical consumer goods available for distribution

In case it became necessary to curtail the volume of money, that could be done through taxation . . . . Only a decrease in the volume of consumer goods, due to famine or disaster, would necessitate a decrease in the volume of money . . . . If price levels are too low, too large a share of the products goes to satisfy those who own claims on the fixed assets and those engaged in actual production receive less than would enable them to consume the products of industry. After the desired price level is reached, money should be paid into the stream by the Monetary Trusteeship, only as goods appear ready for distribution, which goods cannot be moved into consumption

---

[17] *The Root of All Evil*, pp. 53, 54.

at the existing price levels without additional money. Given an adequate supply of money, the volume of goods distributable at a given price level would be limited only by the capacity of the nation to produce goods. The volume of goods produced would be limited only by the amount of natural resources, fixed capital, and the number of workers available . . .. The result would be, *not* a fluctuating dollar as the deceivers shout, but a stable dollar as common sense proves. Stability means *constant purchasing power* of a dollar in terms of things people buy . . .. The national Monetary Trustees would be required to file for publication, once a month, an intelligible and easily understood report, which would indicate exactly how much currency was outstanding as at that date . . .. At any time currency was issued, the exact amounts and exactly to whom and how issued would be made public information. There is no reason why such reports could not be simple and understandable to everyone.[18]

The Monetary Trustees should be exclusively full citizens of the country, should have an unblemished record for honesty and integrity and should have had no connection with international banking, either as owners, partners, employees or advisers. They should receive adequate salaries, but should benefit in no way whatsoever, except as citizens of the country, in the amount of money added to or withdrawn from the money stream.[19]

Mr. A. N. Field treats of stability of price level in connection with the exchange rate with Great Britain. " Up to 1914," he writes, "our New Zealand pound was tied up very closely with the British sterling pound: one could always be obtained for the other with very small fluctuation in the rate of exchange.

In August, 1914, the British pound became inconvertible paper and the New Zealand pound followed suit. The exchange rate remained pretty constant between the two until the slump set in. The banks then gradually let the rate widen to 10%, and then in January, 1933, the government put it up to 25%. At this point it has since been held, except for one very slight reduction.[20] The fixed exchange policy was thus broken between 1931 and 1933, but thereafter it was resumed on a different level. This fixed exchange money policy means that if commodity prices in Britain remain steady, commodity prices in New Zealand also remain steady. If British prices fluctuate violently—as they have done to a ruinous extent—New Zealand prices must also fluctuate with equal violence. That is the position so long

---

[18] *Money Creators*, pp. 251, 252, 254, 255, 338.

[19] *Money Creators*, p. 250.

[20] For the advantages to New Zealand of the higher exchange rate, cf. *Money*, by Professor Alfred O'Rahilly, pp. 404–409, 423.

as the one monetary unit is freely exchangeable for the other at a fixed rate. At present the fixed rate remains, but exchange is prohibited.

"The alternative monetary policy to a fixed exchange is to regulate the supply of money in New Zealand to maintain a steady internal price level, and let the exchange rate fluctuate as the outside price level fluctuates. Low prices in Britain would then mean a low exchange rate. Exported produce would bring, all the time, a steadier price in our money. Money would thus be made a much more accurate measure of value than it now is. This would naturally mean a reduction of financial anxiety and worry for everyone exchanging goods and services in return for money payments, which is practically everybody. If the people maintained production, the money end would take care of itself. This is the most urgently needed social reform in the world.

"The banks in the past have regulated the quantity of money in circulation so as to be able to deliver sterling on demand at the fixed rate of exchange . . . .. Methods of regulation would suffice to maintain a steady internal price level. Those controlling the issue of money, instead of watching the exchange rate, would simply watch the various price indices now compiled and any additional ones they thought necessary to have compiled. If prices started rising above the point fixed, money would be withdrawn from circulation: if prices began to fall, more money would be got into circulation. This is done all the time now. To vary the circulation of money, interest rates on overdrafts and fixed deposits are altered; bank advances are contracted or expanded . . . .. In controlling money to keep the price level steady no attempt would be made to control the price of individual commodities.[21] What would be done would be, in effect, to make up a market basketful of stable commodities, the quantity of each article in the basket being in proportion to the quantity passing in trade. The objective would then be so to regulate the value of money in circulation that a New Zealand pound note would, as nearly as possible, always buy this basketful. Flour might be up, butter down, and every item moving according to demand and supply, but, averaged over the lot, possession of a pound note would enable its holder to walk home with just about the same total basketful all the time.

---

[21] What is said here by Mr. Field in *The Truth about New Zealand* must be supplemented by the teaching of Pope Pius XI in *Quadragesimo Anno* on the role of vocational groups. When the guilds or vocational groups are organized and functioning under a state charter, the activities of the groups will be directed to the common good and they will strive to arrive at just prices for the goods or services they furnish. The state will exercise supreme control.

"Stabilizing money takes the money factor out of price fluctuations, and leaves just the non-monetary factors of demand and supply of commodities. As one well-known writer on these subjects has pointed out, the money factor is like the tides of the ocean, and the commodity demand-and-supply factor is like the waves of the sea, bobbing up and down to different levels all the time. The tides are the big factor determining the level of the water, and the waves a comparatively small factor, even in the greatest storm. The money factor is like the tides, and is the principal thing determining the price level. If it is got under control we can have a stability and a prosperity in industry that we can never know today."

Mr. Field then shows by means of index figures the practical working on the exchange rate with London of a stabilized price level in New Zealand and adds that the effect of the exchange movement would be to iron out price fluctuation to a large extent. He concludes the chapter with the observation that "stability in internal purchasing power is the only sensible basis on which to control money. Money must be made a just measure of value. If it is not, every money transaction perpetrates injustice, with debts on one level and prices of commodities on another level. Injustice sooner or later means the disintegration of the existing social order."

Some important remarks on this aspect of national monetary reform are to be found in *Minority Report No. III of the Irish Banking Commission* (1938), drawn up by Mr. P. J. O'Loughlen. In chapter 1 of his report and in his Appendix II, Mr. O'Loughlen stresses the fundamental disorder of modern economic life, which has been so much insisted on in this book, namely, the subordination of members of Christ to production and of production to finance, or, to put it more succinctly, the domination of money over society. After a brief allusion to the foundation of twenty-six central banks in twenty-six different countries, affiliated to the Bank for International Settlements established at Basle, he quotes from the *Majority Report*, from which he is a dissentient, the following statement on the functions of a central bank. "The principal duty of a central bank is to maintain the integrity of the national monetary unit. To carry out this task the central bank has to ensure the maintenance of external stability (in terms of gold, or sterling, or some other currency), and to take care of the monetary reserves of gold or foreign exchange, and also to have certain means to influence the currency and credit position within the country." Mr. O'Loughlen then adds: "The objective of monetary policy, here so plainly stated, namely, the control or restriction of currency and credit within the country, appears to me to be one in which the interests of bondholders, and those who trade in money, are given complete precedence, and the interests of the ordinary people in each country, who need remunerative employment above all else, are considered to be of a very minor importance. I have already stated my view that the currency and credit position within the country should reflect its own power to produce wealth, its capacity for development, and the necessity to provide employment for its people. It is the stated view of my colleagues (of the *Majority Report*) that these things . . .are secondary considerations and should be sacrificed to maintain a fixed foreign exchange rate."

Now, the maintenance of stability in purchasing power of national exchange media has not been a *desideratum* wherever the money power has exercised domination over society. In fact money has come to dominate, as we have seen, largely through the disregard of this indispensable condition of the just functioning of an exchange medium. Mr. O'Loughlen rightly insists upon aiming at stability of the price level in view of reversing the present disorder. "Owing to our attaching the Irish currency to that of Great Britain," he writes, " prices in Ireland have been determined hitherto by the prices ruling in England, with disastrous results for Irish agriculture . . .. As agriculture will have to keep its costs down to the lowest possible level in order to retain its market in England, all hope of either a rising standard of living, or of an increasing internal market, will be in vain; and in vain also, will be any hope of increased employment in the rural areas . . .. Self-government does not consist in having a flag and the trappings and appearance of independence, but in having effective control over vital national interests. We have been persuaded by the Banking Commission of 1926 to relinquish all but the appearance of control over such important and vital national interests as our price level." But there is no special validity attaching to any particular price level. The price level for any country is the level at which that particular country is best able to attain and maintain the fullest possible use of its resources. As the circumstances vary within wide limits, the levels of prices at which they will be able to maintain full employment will vary also. The maintenance of fixed rates of foreign exchange tends to force the prices in different countries to conform to a common level, thus preventing the development of price levels which are most conducive to the maintenance of full employment, and a remunerative return for industry.

"It is quite practicable to develop such levels of wages and prices within a particular country as are most conducive to the common good, and the appropriate, and indeed the only, means by which such a policy can be carried out is a national monetary system which has regard principally to the internal conditions of the country in which it operates, and which is directed to the maintenance of full employment for productive purposes, and also of such prices and wages as are most conducive to national well being. On the other hand, a monetary system which aims at being international and which, by maintaining fixed rates of foreign exchange, forces internal conditions to accord with those of other countries, precludes us from adopting measures which would enable remunerative prices, or wages on which people can live in decent comfort, being realized in practical daily life.

"If a fixed rate of foreign exchange is abandoned, and a policy of the internal development and use of all our resources is followed, there is no reason whatever to apprehend any wide or constant fluctuations of the exchange rates. As between England and ourselves, the movements of the exchange rate would correspond with movements in the level of prices in the two countries and price levels, apart from abnormal conditions such as another war, will tend to move slowly and gradually. My proposals would not introduce wide or rapid fluctuations of prices in Ireland; but would allow the two countries to adjust themselves to each other in accordance with their respective purchasing power, which would not be subject to any greater condition of instability than at present. Not only is this the case but active steps could and should be taken by the Irish monetary authorities to minimize such inconvenience to importers and exporters as a moving rate of exchange may otherwise bring by taking appropriate steps for this purpose. These steps should be:

(1) To establish and maintain a forward market for foreign exchange in Ireland.

(2) To provide and control an equalization fund, designed not to peg the rate of exchange at an arbitrary level, but to render as gradual as possible any movements of exchange rates which were the results of an active policy of internal development.

In Appendix I, I have outlined the character and scope of an Economic Development Commission which would be able to organize and to direct the unused productive resources of the nation, with the object of maintaining full employment, and so raising the standards of economic life. . . An effective balance between expansion and contraction of the volume of money would require to be maintained by the Economic Development Commission. The practicable daily test of the fluctuations of such a balance would be the maintenance of a constant and equal activity of the country's production and consumption, as disclosed by statistical indices [to be compiled by the Economic Development Commission], and the absence of any considerable degree of unemployment . . .. The Economic Development Commission should be in close touch with the Currency Commission, the Department of Finance, and the banks, and should be represented on the Foreign Exchange Committee which I recommend should be established."[22]

In the pamphlet, *The Arch-Enemy of Economic Freedom,* Professor Soddy treats of some points not explicitly mentioned in his previous works. He deals excellently with the remedy proposed by some monetary reformers, namely, the closing of the price gap so as to be fair to both producers and consumers. He also explains very clearly how to face the difficulty of investments in foreign countries. He examines the Morgenthau and Keynes Plans. Following Mr. McNair Wilson, he insists that stabilization of the internal price level is the national policy required in every country, whereas, "the fixation of the foreign exchanges, which means continual seesawing of the internal price level, is favored by all the megalomaniacs, who, whether from too optimistic humanitarian dreams or personal egotism, labor 'planning' on a world scale, and a premature attempt to unite all nations into one-world state with an international currency, in the belief, apparently, that a lie can become true if it is made universal . . .. A premature move in the direction of world unification would endanger the nations losing such autonomy as now remains to them and the whole world would be dominated by the dictatorship of those who only seek power over the lives and labors of others." Professor Soddy here re-echoes the warning contained in *A Twentieth Century Economic System,* namely, that a Central International Bank must not be entrusted with the task of keeping the imports and exports of member nations in equilibrium. Multilateral trade could be provided for by the Exchange Controls of the participating nations having representatives at an International Exchange or Clearing House, but each nation must have charge of maintaining its own imports and exports in equilibrium. "If a Central International Bank were entrusted with this task instead of each nation being free to solve its own domestic problem in its own way, we should be once more back to the old condition of financial war to control a central monetary authority which, in its turn, would control the domestic affairs of so-called independent nations."

Money or token wealth, as we have seen, is destined by its nature to facilitate exchanges, so that the persons composing the families of a given unit or area may more easily be able to provide themselves with the necessities of life—food, clothes and shelter. Exchanges are, therefore, subordinate to this main purpose and " exchanges between nations situated all over the world (the establishment of which may be highly advantageous)

---

[22] *Minority Report No. III,* by Mr. P. J. O'Loughlen, pp. 26, 42, 45, 50.

are by their nature subsidiary both to the local development of wealth for the locality and to local exchange.[23] Local development must aim at avoiding waste and at being as full as possible, subject to the overriding requirements of personal freedom, family life and the properties of the soil. " It is common to hear nowadays that *because* Great Britain is a small island very densely populated, and *because* during the war we have sacrificed so many of our foreign securities, *therefore*, we must make it our first business to develop our foreign trade. The logic of this argument (and it is applied to many other countries besides Great Britain) has never been explained. Common sense with an eye upon primaries would hold that *because* our country is densely populated and likely to feel the pinch of poverty, *therefore* we should apply ourselves to an intense local production (always governed by the dictates of the soil) and to internal exchanges, and thus provide our primary economic needs in the most economical way with as little dissipation as possible of our real wealth abroad. Such a general policy would ensure at once the provision of necessities before luxuries and the fullest possible use of the talents and initiative of our people.[24] The excellent article in *The Weekly Review,* from which we have just been quoting, was occasioned by a recently published *Statement of Principles for an International Monetary Fund.* Concerning this statement the article says: "The International Monetary Proposals, whatever their technical merits or defects may be (and a Committee of financial experts in control of an international fund must cause some concern as being the opposite pole from anything like a democratic or even national system), deal only with the machinery of an activity [the manipulation of international exchange medium] two removes from primary economics . . . .. From this it follows that no economic utopia can be expected to result from the joint statement of the financial experts; it tends rather to tighten the grip that a few non-national financiers have upon the world."

---

[23] Article on money in *The Weekly Review*, April 27, 1944.
[24] Ibid..

CHAPTER NINE
THE FULL RETURN TO ORDER

How have the two evils deplored by Professor Soddy and so many others, namely, the domination of finance over politics and economics and the instability of national price levels become so widespread? In this, as in other cases, the ultimate reason is to be found in the refusal of men to submit to the Divine Plan for Order in the world through the Mystical Body of Christ. In spite of the naturalistic opposition of the Jewish nation to the supernatural Messias and to his plan for order, and notwithstanding the weakness of fallen human nature, Western Europe in the thirteenth century had come to acknowledge God's rights in the way He Himself had laid down and had organized society on the basis that man's supreme dignity was his supernatural and supernational life as a member of Christ. The truth was recognized that all men were members of Christ, actual or potential, and that society, as such, was bound to favor membership of Christ. The guilds of the Middle Ages were an application of this great doctrine of human solidarity in Christ to economic affairs. Social life, in which politics and economics would be put into watertight compartments and sectioned off from the life of members of Christ was completely alien to the minds of that day. Western Europe as a whole then recognized the authority of the Vicar of Christ the King, and his right to say what was moral or immoral in politics and economics. As far back as the Council of Nicaea (325), in which the divinity of the head of the Mystical Body was defined, the Church had declared war on usury. The domination of finance over politics and economics had proved disastrous for the Roman Empire, just as it is proving disastrous for states in our own times.

Accordingly, in spite of deficiencies and imperfections, the society of Western Europe down to the sixteenth century was organized under the banner of Christ the King and accepted the fact that there was a moral law binding on financiers, as well as on politicians and economists. The revolt of the sixteenth century sectioned off the Christian life from the life of the citizen, so political and economic organization left membership of Christ out of account. According to the Catholic ideal, the one divinely instituted ideal, the whole life of a member of Christ is meant to be subject to Christ and animated with the meritorious supernatural life of grace, just as all the movements of the hand or of any other member are subject to the head in the physical body. In addition, there is solidarity between the members of the Mystical Body as there is between the members of the physical body. According to the Lutheran ideal, all the activity of a Christian in the world is withdrawn from the rule of Christ and given over to Naturalism.

Lutheranism, then, initiated that dualism, which separates life into two halves so independent that they have only accidental relations with each other, and thus prepared the way for Liberalism. Liberalism is simply the application of Naturalism to morality, politics, economics, and finance. Perhaps we may best describe it by saying that it consists in erecting particular sections of human activity, economic or political, into separate domains, each with its own autonomous end completely independent of the final end of man as a member of Christ. Thus when politics and economics were withdrawn from subjection to the moral law binding on members of Christ, the manipulation of money or exchange medium was in due course withdrawn from subjection to politics and economics and erected into an autonomous department of life subject only to its own laws. The Nominalist philosophy of Locke, the philosopher of the Bank of England, favored the same tendency. "At the time the new social order was beginning," writes Pope Pius XI in the Encyclical Letter, *Quadragesimo Anno*, "the doctrines of rationalism had already taken firm hold of large numbers, and an economic science alien to the true moral law had soon arisen, whence it followed that free rein was given to human avarice." The Catholic Church, guided by the Holy Ghost, sees far ahead. —*Locke's Essay Concerning Human Understanding* and *Mill's Principles of Political Economy* are on the Index.[1]

The rending of the Mystical Body by the so-called Reformation movement and the uprise of private judgment or individualism on the supernatural level, led inevitably to the breaking up of the guild organization and to the uprise of individualism, that is, of unbridled self-seeking, on the natural level of production, distribution and exchange of material goods. In his work on *The Economic Effects of the Reformation*, Professor George O'Brien has shown the effect of the Calvinist or Puritan doctrine of success in life as a sign of man's predestination. The result of the unlimited competition, unscrupulous underselling and feverish advertising,

---

[1] For the development of these ideas see *The Mystical Body of Christ and the Reorganization of Society* and *The Workingmen's Guilds of the Middle Ages*.

was inevitably the subordination of human beings to production. " The new conception of Christianity," writes Father Eustace Dudley,[2] "which replaced the old ideal, taught a radically different doctrine regarding the relation of this life to the next, and particularly as regards the value and purpose of good works and moral living. It was a doctrine that centered the whole of man's energy on the successful fulfillment of his vocation as a sure proof of his election; and which whilst it produced a prudent painstaking type of Christian with a great passion for duty, yet rendered impossible the fulfillment of his duties towards his weaker brethren. Believing as he did, and supported in his belief by the political economists of the time, that his own enlightened selfishness was productive of the highest happiness for the greatest number, he soon came to classify the poor and less fortunate as the product of laziness and vice; and they, neglected and forgotten, became either the victims of capitalism or were hidden away in state institutions under the stigma of poverty." The self-centered economic theories of Calvinism replaced the self-sacrificing asceticism of members of Christ. The aim of society became not to supply a sufficiency of goods to families, so that the human personality of their members might be cultivated to the utmost, but to produce as much as possible irrespective of the deleterious effects on the personality of the workers engaged in production.

But the subjection of human personality to the production of material goods is not the end of the perversion of order. There is a further stage of decay, which is realized by the subordination of the production of real wealth to the manipulation of exchange medium or token wealth. Gradually, finance came to occupy the disordered dominant position it holds today. In his work *Die Juden und das Wirtschaftsleben*, the first edition of which appeared in 1911, Professor Werner Sombart aptly sums up the situation as follows: "If we want to make clear in one sentence the direction in which modern political economy is moving, we can say: the stock exchange agents of the banks are becoming, in an ever-increasing measure, the dictators of economic life. All economic happenings are more and more subordinate to the decisions of finance. The question whether a new industrial undertaking is to spring up or an existing one to be developed; whether the owner of a shop or a store is to get the means to extend his business, all these questions are decided in the offices of banks and bankers. In just the same way the sale of products is becoming, in an ever-greater degree, a problem of finance. Our greatest industries are indeed already just as much financial associations as industrial undertakings." Leadership amongst financial, industrial and commercial interests has thus passed to the powerful groups which have secured "a monopoly in the creation of

---

[2] *National Resurrection*, pp. 49–50.

national credit, and these groups, being internationally organized, have only to be left free in order to dominate the earth.[3]

The collectivist reaction against Liberalism and laissez-faire has not attempted to undo the fundamental disorder whereby family life and the soil of the earth are sacrificed for industry and commerce, and industry and commerce are subordinated to finance. On the contrary, "Today we see taking shape what promises to be one of the most amazing compromises of history—the courtship and impending union of finance capitalism and socialism in the bonds of an unholy matrimony. The high contracting parties have apparently drawn up their ante-nuptial contract; at any rate they seem to be agreed upon such measures of collectivization—sometimes politely called nationalization—as may be necessary to wipe out the small units in industry and commerce. Larger units not amenable to discipline will be socialized outright; others will be merged in huge monopolies, bureaucratically planned. The small manufacturer will surrender his independent status to become a minor functionary in some official or semi-official industrial combine; the small shopkeeper will pull down his shutters to become a counter-hand in a sort of universal chain store.[4]

Fallen man cannot maintain the rule of reason over the senses and observe order in social life, unless he subjects his reason to God and acknowledges Our Lord Jesus Christ and his Divine Plan for world order. According to the hierarchical order of the practical sciences, the art of manipulating money is subordinate to economics, the science which, according to Saint Thomas, studies families in the constituent relations of their members and in their conditions of existence, and to politics, the science which has for object the organization of the state in view of the complete common good of the families and persons composing it. Decisions as to what is for the common good of the state and family life must be made, not by those skilled in the manipulation of money but by those in charge of the common good and of the maintenance of sound family life. Those skilled in the manipulation of money are masters of an auxiliary art furnishing to politics and economics the instrument they need. The revolt against the supernatural life and the Divine Plan for Order and the withdrawal of politics and economics from subjection to the Mystical Body of Christ have gradually led to the overthrow of the natural hierarchical order of the practical sciences. Money now rules. Those skilled in manipulating it dictate policy to statesmen and economists. Combines and monopolies oust small family businesses; farming is treated as an industry to be mechanized in imitation of the factory, and the land,

---

[3] Article in *The Weekly Review*, May 11, 1944, by A. K. Chesterton.

[4] Ibid. In a word, men will be treated as mere individuals, not as persons.

the source of the necessaries of life, is exhausted. The results are apparent everywhere in the decay of family life and the loss of soil fertility. The proper functioning of money is not a panacea for all disorders, as is clear from all I have written here and elsewhere, but its improper functioning is even more disastrous nowadays than it was in the days of the Roman Empire. The pace of life (and of destruction) has been accelerated by modern inventions.

The Beveridge Report in England does not aim at undoing the disordered domination of finance. On the contrary, it accepts the dictation of finance over industry and, acquiescing in that reversal of order, it tends to promote the return of the Servile State, by the introduction of compulsion and by nationalization of the majority of the medical profession.[5] An excellent pamphlet by the Public Relations Committee of the Belfast Division of the B.M.A. points out that the basic proposal of the White Paper on a National Health Service (February, 1944) is "A Central Employment Board for Doctors." "Under the proposed Social Security plan," the pamphlet states, "disability benefit is to be paid to insured persons, so long as the disability lasts, subject to acceptance of medical treatment. Thus in future a patient may be faced with the alternative of taking his doctor's advice (or orders ?) or losing the disability benefit for

---

[5] "(Beveridge) does not stress in his report all the sanctions and disciplines, and even coercions, which the implementation of Social Security will actually involve, but they are implicit" (*Insurance for All and Everything*, by R. Davison, quoted by Rev, L. Watt, S.J., in *A Catholic View of the Beveridge Plan*, p. 8.

That part of the Beveridge Plan which would lead to the nationalization of the greater part of the medical profession is manifestly unjust to the public as well as to the doctors themselves. The services of the few medical practitioners not forced to become state servants would be available only to the rich. The remaining doctors would lose their independence and their initiative, with deplorable consequences to the future of their profession. It is barely credible that the planners can really believe that the services which doctors now render to the public will be maintained under state control " (*Our Peace Crisis*, by Arthur Rogers). Cf. *Barrier to Health*, by Douglas Boyd (The Abbey Press, Bangor, Co. Down, Ireland).

The booklet, *Our Peace Crisis*, by Arthur Rogers, published by the Sterling Press, 38 Bedford Street, London W.C.2., contains excellent information about the groups that are planning for the increase of state control. Information about PEP (Political and Economic Planning Group) was given years ago, in *All These Things* (1936) and *Facts about the Ban*, of England (1937), by A. N. Field, New Zealand.

which he has been taxed. Strict control of medical certification means, of course, disciplinary measures against the doctors who err too often in favor of the patient and the opening of personal medical records to a government department, in a position to give an absolute ruling, which cannot be questioned in the courts of justice. To aid in the detection of malingering the number of 'sick visitors' to be increased .... No provision is made in the document for the medical profession, organized in a service, to remain free to express advice and views to Parliament and the public. Criticism, however needed to ventilate individual grievances, would become 'politics.' . . .. On certain matters, the all important ones of policy, the decision of the Minister is to be final. As regards disciplinary measures, there is to be no questioning his judgment in the courts of law. Not only is the Central Board, under the aegis of the Minister, to have the above powers, but it will have the power to move doctors about from one part of the country to another . . .. He who gives up freedom seeking security soon loses both freedom and security."

Another pamphlet, entitled *The Political Planners*, by the same body, on the same subject, says: "There is a growing suspicion, within the medical profession. . . that the White Paper's proposals were originally inspired by a desire to control an independent profession in order to safeguard medical certification on behalf of a Treasury indirectly paying out sickness benefits from a special Social Insurance Fund. Today the medical profession is awakened to the dangers of a Treasury conditioned outlook . . .. The British Medical Association is against the submergence of the individual in an authoritarian state such as we are fighting against today in all the battlefields of the War." The domination of finance is to be used to attack family life in another way also, in order to "oil the wheels of industry.[6] "In the promotion of the cause of social servitude," writes Arthur Rogers in *Our Peace Crisis* (p. 38), "the Beveridge Report has as its companion the Education Bill, brought in by Mr. R. A. Butler in December, 1943, the object of which is a general reorganization of education." "The children of today, and the unborn, will, as the human elements essential to our economic supremacy, be bent, toughened and trained in the New Educational System: through physical training, intensified school medical

---

[6] 'The phrase is quoted from Mr. R. A. Butler, by Mr. C. I. Kelly in *The Catholic Times*, May 26, 1944. It is clear from Mr. Kelly's excellent article that the Education Bill is part of the preparation for another attempt to outstrip other nations in what has been misnamed " a favorable balance of trade." This new effort to galvanize industrialism will have disastrous effects on farming and, as in the past, will set up that tension which makes war inevitable.

services, midday meals at school (mothers at work). Their parents must not interfere.[7]

In *Our Peace Crisis* (pp. 86, 93, 94, 95), Arthur Rogers insists also upon the naturalism or anti-supernaturalism of many of those engaged in postwar planning in England. "It will not be enough, he writes, "to stop the two-pronged advance of the Beveridge and Butler Panzer Divisions, now developing into a menacing pincer movement. We must face the fact that, at present, the British nation is being actually planned out of existence. The restoration of the family, with the father its head and the mother its heart, is an absolute necessity. This point of policy touches upon most other matters of social policy and many matters of economic policy. It is not possible that the original instigators of current policies and proposals ... believe in man's fall from [the supernatural life of] grace . . .. his is not altogether surprising. In Great Britain, as in other countries, a small minority of individuals—determined and powerful—

---

[7] Article by Mr. C. I. Kelly in *The Catholic Times*, May 26, 1944.

It is well to add that the English White Paper on Employment recently issued, explicitly proposes to continue the pre-war ruinous policy towards farming. It states that, "we must continue to import from abroad a large proportion of our foodstuffs and raw materials and to a greater extent than ever before we shall have to pay for them by the export of our goods and services." Commenting, in *The Weekly Review*, September 7th, 1944, on a recent pronouncement of the British Minister for Agriculture to the effect that agriculture will do well "for some years to come," Mr. A. K. Chesterton asks why the Minister does not promise that farming will continue to flourish. Though English agriculture has been increased by over 70%, since the beginning of the war and has been restored to something like its former prosperity, yet the country is "still a long way from being able to meet its own needs." "The answer is," Mr. Chesterton continues, "that as soon as the last gun is fired the whole immense might of the City of London will be directed to the task of securing new foreign bonds to replace the old which the war swallowed. And to achieve this end the lenders of money abroad will desire to wave the bait of the British market before the eyes of agrarian countries, as well as to ensure that their interest will continue to arrive in the traditional form of foreign foodstuffs. On that account, beyond any doubt whatever, foreign foodstuffs will be allowed to flood into this country the moment the war ends, and an attempt will be made to buy off the British farmers wrath by promising him a share of the newly liberated markets . . .. What makes the position even more grotesque is that the game of foreign lending is very nearly played out."

reject the Christian view of the nature of man, believing stubbornly in the diametrically opposite view that it is within the power of man to become as God, through his own material knowledge. It is among those who hold this belief—which is the apotheosis of materialism, and which some call the serpent cult, or Satanism—that there are people who aspire to a millennium which they believe to be attainable through their becoming themselves the masters of mankind. Such people promote socialism and kindred forms of materialistic religion, also class hatred, revolutions and wars, as agencies of destruction; and there can be no doubt that it is in their philosophy that the 'planning' movement has its first origin . . .. From a denial of original sin . . .it is but a short step to acceptance of the view that man is an evolving being, who is perpetually improving or progressing . . .. Those who hold this view are identifiable by their references to 'progress,' made without any indication, or apparent thought, of the goal to which man is, as they say, 'progressing' or of the end for which man is made. Judging from their plans and their arguments, it is safe to assume that nearly all our leading planners are 'progressives,' rather than instructed Christians, where they are not actively anti-Christian."

It was the conviction of their membership of Christ that nerved the early Christians for the long struggle for order under the Roman Empire. That same conviction shared in and acted upon by all Catholics the world over will be necessary to undo the present reversal of order in economic organization. The first fruit of that conviction ought to be the demand by Catholics of all nations that the political, economic and financial arrangements between states at the end of the present conflict shall be submitted, as to their morality, to the judgment of the Sovereign Pontiff, the Vicar of Christ.

APPENDIX I
MONEY—BANK—DEPOSIT

The following explanations of the above terms from the pen of Professor O'Rahilly, the distinguished President of University College, Cork, will, I am sure, be useful to my readers.

MONEY—"Money as such—apart from its material record—is something immaterial: it is a moral and legal relationship, something instituted by man, and hence not existing in nature or in the animal world. It is a socially recognized right-to-buy transferable from one person to another. It is not made out of anything: it is just issued or created, just as a person makes a promise or creates a contractual relationship. The state, representing the community, issues money, which is usually recorded on bits of paper or pieces of metal, but may be recorded merely by a few figures in ink on the books of the central bank. The banks issue money by bank notes and still more by mere entries on their books, which we transfer to one another by checks, i.e., by directing the banker to alter his book entries" (*The Standard*, April, 17 1942).

BANK— "A bank nowadays is an institution which, on the basis of a proportion of state money created by the central bank, creates another and more convenient form of money (transferable by check) for the government as well as for individuals or firms . . .. The banks are public utility institutions, exercising the communally delegated function of creating (and canceling) the money required by the community. They are entitled only to a strictly controlled service charge; and when the service is provided for the state itself (or for public works), the charge may well be 'nil or even negative,'" (*The Standard*, Oct. 1, 1943).

DEPOSIT—"Deposit has an entirely different meaning today from *depositum*, just as the word bank itself has changed its meaning. In Roman Law, *depositum* means anything entrusted for safekeeping to another who does not acquire any property in the thing. It can be translated a bailment or—to invent a new term—an entrust. This primitive function still subsists in modern banks—in the plate, jewelry, securities, etc., kept in a banker's safe or strong-room . . .. Nowadays a deposit is the liability of the banker to pay a sum on demand, a right of action which he has created against himself in order to purchase an asset or counter-claim. It is not a *depositum*, it is not the cash in reserve, it is not some thing or some value entrusted to the banker as bailee. Even if the customer lodges legal tender, this is not a *depositum* but what in Latin is called a *mutuum*, i.e., a loan... A 'deposit' no longer means a *depositum,* but a debt" (*Money*, pp. 48, 49, 70).

APPENDIX II
GARDENS, FERTILIZERS, AND FINANCE

An excellent little book, entitled *The Compost Gardener*, has been written by Mr. F. C. King, at the suggestion and with the aid of that eminent authority on farming and the care of the land, Sir Albert Howard. Sir Albert says in the Introduction that it was one of the compensations he had for having to evacuate his home in 1940 that he was able to make the acquaintance of Mr. F. C. King, a head gardener of twenty-five years' experience in Westmoreland.[1]

The book is essentially practical and consists of Mr. King's lectures on how best to grow about twenty-five ordinary vegetables: cabbage, broccoli, carrots, parsnips, onions, etc., etc. These lectures, however, are unusual; unusual because based on the natural order, which has been overthrown by the disorder consequent upon the domination of finance and paper costs in modern life. The natural order demands that to have healthy human beings, the animals and plants upon which the human beings feed must be healthy. In order that the animals may be healthy, the plants, by which they are nourished, must be healthy. The health of the series therefore starts with the health of the soil, on which the plants grow. "When we compare our efforts with those of nature," writes the author, "it is obvious that there is something seriously wrong somewhere with a system of cultivation which robs plants of their natural birthright—health—and makes it imperative either continually to change our stock of plants or to employ poison sprays to protect them from pests and disease . . .. In my judgment the first condition of successful gardening is to build up soil fertility. The appearance of pests or disease is a warning that our soil needs attention and that steps should at once be taken to correct this state of affairs by seeing that the vegetable wastes of the garden are converted into humus and returned to the soil. Our crops will then be provided with a store of balanced food . . .. The problem of manuring is simple. All we have to do is to supply the earthworm and the invisible labor force—moulds and microbes—with the humus they need. The waste products of these unseen workers then feed the crop... As the fertility of our soil is built up, pests and diseases disappear, because once the soil is fertile the crops protect themselves . . .. I have used many tons of compost and have been impressed by the almost total absence of pests such as wireworms and slugs . . .. I am convinced, after years of observation, that crops would give

---

[1] *The Compost Gardener* is published by T. Wilson and Son, Ltd., High-gate, Kendal, Westmoreland.

heavier yields if we were not so keen on depriving the soil of waste vegetable matter and on poisoning the soil by the use of fungicides and insecticides."

Sir Albert Howard contributes a very useful chapter on *Compost and its Preparation*. "The operations of nature," he writes, "are based on humus. Nature never provides artificial manures to stimulate growth or poison sprays to destroy insect and fungous diseases. If we copy Nature in our gardening we can make our garden manure itself and also produce crops which are not only resistant to pests, but also transmit disease resistance and health to ourselves. This, in brief, is the basis of organic gardening."

The book, too, contains a fine section on how to prepare and cook vegetables, contributed by Mrs. Gordon Grant, whose work, *Feeding the Family in War Time*, is published by George G. Harrap & Co., Ltd.

INORGANIC FERTILIZERS

"Commercial manures," writes Mr. King, "may be roughly divided into two classes: organic and mineral. In my opinion the sparing use of the organic class [Fish meal, bones, rape meal, etc.] will often give beneficial results for a time, but there is no place for mineral inorganic fertilizers in a well-conducted garden." He then goes on to speak of the deleterious effects of nitrate of soda, sulphate of ammonia, basic slag, super-phosphate of lime, and the potassic manures—kainit, sulphate of potash, etc. With regard to basic slag and super-phosphate of lime, he says: "I have used considerable quantities of both and was quite satisfied at the time that I had done a wise thing; now I am patiently retracing my steps and building up the fertility of the soil under my charge on a surer foundation. The good effects from the use of these artificials were not maintained and the deterioration of the land was so marked that I had no option but to discontinue their use . . .. If the land is treated with artificial manures, we encourage pests and disease. To control these, more poisonous substances are used in the form of washes and powders, thereby producing the death of the inhabitants of the soil which alone make and maintain soil fertility." Mr. King strongly recommends the use of sewage sludge and says that it is far better than even farmyard manure.

On the other hand, both basic slag and super-phosphate of lime are recommended for grasslands in *Ley Farming*, by Sir. R. George Stapledon and William Davies (Penguin Series), and in *Back to Better Grass*, by I. G. Lewis (Faber and Faber, Ltd.), as well as in *Soil and Sense*, by Michael Graham (Faber and Faber, Ltd.).

The Earl of Portsmouth (Viscount Lymington) in *Famine in England*

(H. F. and G. Witherby, Ltd.) seems to sum up the situation excellently. "The farmer," he writes, "having exhausted his soil, has often tried to repair the loss, not by the relatively costly business of good mixed farming, but by artificial manures. Appropriately enough, the artificial manure-maker is the manufacturer of high explosives, so what he gains on the swings of war he can keep on the roundabouts of peace. The reckless use of artificial manure is as destructive as the careless handling of explosives . . .. Artificial manures may be useful in exceptional cases to stimulate production, or as with basic slag to help derelict grassland, but unless they are used in conjunction with good farming they are highly dangerous. The processes of life depend as much on decay as on growth. Healthy growth can only take place when there has been proper decay of organic matter, which becomes humus. This can only be brought about by the working of soil bacteria. Reckless use of sulphate of ammonia, nitro-chalk, potash and other salts kills the bacteria, and so the plant cannot remain healthy when there is no humus in the soil. Thus the overdosing of badly farmed soil with artificial manure can complete the ruin, which the endless cereal crops and cutting of forests have started."[2]

It may be well to add a few words on the question of the use of sprays from another distinguished farmer and writer, Lord Northbourne. In *Look to the Land* he writes, "If there is any doubt as to whether artificial manures ought to be classed as poisons there can be no doubt about the classification of the ever increasing array of sprays which are applied to crops in order to kill pests. These are frankly poisonous. Arsenic, lead, copper, tar, oils, nicotine are freely used. They all get to the ground in the end, and what they do there, or even before they get there, nobody knows. True, plants continue to grow on the ground, but why is it that more and more spraying is necessary?[3]

---

[2] Lime, phosphate and potash sometimes have important places in the land's constitution, but they and the nitrogen manures, play only a small part in feeding it . . .. Artificial manures are no substitute for dung because they provide no humus" (*Soil and Sense*, pp. 96–97).

It has been established that the soil fraction which is the chief carrier of fertility is the humus. This is produced by the decay of plant structures and is assisted by the addition of animal wastes " (*The Discipline of Peace*, p. 122, by K. E. Barlow, Faber and Faber, Ltd.).

[3] A French-Canadian paper, *L'Echo du Bas Saint Laurent*, 23rd July, 1927, quoted the journal of the American Chemical Society about the effect of the poisonous insecticides used on tobacco plants. The article states that considerable quantities of arsenic, etc., remain in the plants and pass

In the controversy about the use of artificial manures and poison sprays, just as in the controversy about bread and roller-mills, we must not forget the influence of the disordered domination of finance, under which we live, or rather, exist. This disordered domination of finance has been responsible for the ruin of much good land. "International debt and soil erosion," writes Lord Northbourne in *Look to the Land*, "are twin brother and sister, inseparables." Financial forces will favor the use of these substances, because the rhythm of production of them can be accelerated in order to pay interest on debt. Nature's rhythm, however, must be respected with regard to the soil, or else the results will be disastrous.

The disastrous cycle which was begun at the dictation of 'science' and finance has been admirably outlined in an article by C. D. Bachelor in *The Weekly Review*, April 27, 1944.

Nature's method of soil management," he writes, "was practiced by farmers for thousands of years, right up to the time when Baron Liebig made what was acclaimed as a marvelous discovery.[4] He analyzed the ashes of plants and finding that they consisted of nitrogen, phosphates and potash, declared that all that was necessary to grow crops in abundance was to incorporate these three chemicals into the soil and all would do well. His findings, backed up by commerce, very quickly became practiced

---

from there into the systems of smokers.

[4] Rome was living on the tribute of her conquered provinces, just as a modern city lives upon the produce of distant farmlands—often beyond the seas. Rome had, like modern towns, a sewage system that disgorged into rivers and seas . . .. A great German scientist, Baron von Liebig, writing in the year 1840, was perhaps the first man to notice what was happening. He observed that the quantity of minerals in the soil was limited, and that it was possible to measure the extent to which every crop exhausted the earth. That, of course, was on the assumption that there was no return of these minerals. Writing of the Roman system he said that their sewers engulfed, first the agricultural wealth of the Roman peasants, and later that of Sicily, Sardinia, and the once fertile coast of Africa. He saw a similar fate threaten the modern world but at this point his argument took a curious turn. Instead of devising means to return sewage and garbage to the soil, he set his mind to work on substitutes—ersatz food for the earth. He became the father of chemical fertilizers . . .. It is chiefly for lack of a regular return to the soil of organic manure, forming 'humus' that fertile land became dust-bowls and deserts" (*Our Debt to the Soil*, by Reginald Reynolds, in *The Weekly Review*, May 25, 1944).

by farmers and at the present day some millions of tons of chemicals are annually poured into the soil, with the result that the soil is being steadily poisoned, earth worms, fungus and bacteria killed, and the balance of the soil completely upset.

"The introduction of chemical farming soon brought about a censor from nature in the shape of pests and diseases, which attacked both vegetation and soil with disastrous results. Undismayed, the chemists invented sprays, powders and washes—mostly of a poisonous nature—to combat the evil which they instigated.

"The chemists, even now, had not finished their task of destruction, for the food grown on chemicals and sprayed with chemicals soon had an adverse effect upon the health of man who consumed it, with the result that there was, and still is, an unprecedented demand for indigestion cures, stomach powders, nerve tonics, etc., which again fell to the chemists to invent and supply. A casual glance at the advertisements appearing in newspapers, periodicals and on the hoardings will testify to the amount of these patent medicines, which must be consumed by the public.

"To where is this age of chemical farming leading us? There can be but one answer. To the complete destruction of soil fertility, ill-health and suffering amongst mankind and the ultimate starvation of all living things."

ARTIFICIAL MANURES AND FINANCE

I have quoted the statement of the Earl of Portsmouth that the artificial manure-maker is the manufacturer of high explosives, so what he gains on the swings of war he can keep on the roundabouts of peace." An interesting article by H.D.C.P., in *The Weekly Review*, March 2, 1944, enables me to develop that point a little, and to add some further testimony to the effect of artificial manures on the land. "The English farmer," writes H. D. C. P., quoting from *The Times*, "has been urged for the last five years to produce bumper crops at all costs; he has done this, but in doing so he has to take out of the land far more than he has put in.

"In this work he has been very materially assisted by the use of artificial manures. As a small holder myself, and one in constant touch with his farming neighbors, I can say from our corner of England that the verdict is unanimously against the continuance of this crop-snatching policy. Our land is impoverished, and we would never use another artificial again.

"Now there are large vested interests in this drug trade. *Will they be handled after the war in the same way as their companion interests in the armament industry*, or will they be encouraged to survive. The signs of the times in rural market towns are not propitious. The travelers in these things are far from packing up and retiring from the scene of their labors; their directors urge them to greater efforts and the limelight of publicity still shines upon them. That which was a temporary wartime good has all the appearance of becoming a permanent peacetime evil, crops will continue to be snatched until the land of England becomes another 'dustbowl,' and all our food has to be imported from abroad. I have not heard that the directors of the industries concerned in this trade have been warned that their services will be no longer required, and that they are to be classed with the manufacturers of armaments whose efforts must be redirected into the productive works of peace.

"I had written so far when the *Sunday Times* kindly supplied an authoritative postscript in the form of a letter from Sir Albert Howard. He writes: 'The crux of this matter can be stated in a few words. Is the use of artificials and poison sprays, with or without humus, harmful to the soil, to the crops and animals raised thereon and to the health of the human population consuming such produce? After a study of this question in four continents over a period of forty-five years, during which I have had exceptional facilities as an investigator, I am convinced that the answer is: Most emphatically yes. This conclusion is shared by the growing body of pioneers, with whom I am associated. Confirmatory evidence is now coming forward in a torrent . . .. That poison sprays and artificial manures are harmful is proved by a great mass of evidence. Two examples may be quoted. Arsenical washes kill the bees which are essential for pollination, seed formation and the production of honey. Artificials, sulphate of ammonia in particular, destroy earthworms wholesale. These creatures are the great conditioners of food material for healthy crops. Once this important section of the potato grower's unpaid labor force is put out of action, the crops suffer from at least two new diseases—eelworm and virus—and the quality and keeping power of the produce deteriorate. A change over to freshly prepared humus in place of artificials is soon followed by the rapid disappearance of these troubles and by healthy crops.'"

THE IDEAS UNDERLYING THE BIO-DYNAMIC METHOD OF COMPOSTING

Mr. King's book, *The Compost Gardener*, embodies the sound ideas of Sir Albert Howard and the results of his own experiments. In warmly recommending it, and Sir Albert Howard's book, *An Agricultural Testament* (Oxford University Press), the present writer would like to utter a word of warning with regard to the theories associated with the name of Rudolph Steiner and the Anthroposophical Society founded by him. There seems to run through these theories a Kabbalistic deification of man by his natural powers, a pantheistic caricature of our participation in the inner life of God in three divine persons by sanctifying grace.

In 1902, Rudolph Steiner became a member of the Theosophical Society under Mrs. Besant and was Secretary General of the German section until 1913, when he broke away from Mrs. Besant and founded the Anthroposophical Society, a name in all probability derived from a work entitled *Anthroposophia Magica* published about 1650 by the occultist, Thomas Vaughan. Steiner built a temple for the adepts of Anthroposophy at Dornach near Basel in Switzerland. The temple was burned in 1922 but rebuilt. Steiner died in 1925.

According to René Guénon in *Le Theosophisme*, Steiner was a Rosicrucian. Steiner himself defined Anthroposophy as a path of knowledge to guide the spiritual in the human being to the Spiritual in the Universe and so achieve the union of the life-force within man with the universal life-force without, thus forming the deified man. Steiner professed to teach the Spiritual Science by which this inner man could be awakened and brought into contact with the Spirit Beings or Masters who teach and develop man's life-force. According to him the man, Jesus of Nazareth, united himself with one of these Beings and, as a consequence, "mighty forces streamed out from this event as an impulse for all later human development." The student of this Spiritual Science, " by the faculties that are in him, enters consciously the worlds where spiritual beings dwell and spiritual processes take place. He sees spiritual beings and spiritual processes, and he sees too how the beings and the processes of the physical world arise out of the spiritual. It is then his further task to express certain domains of what is revealed to his spiritual sight in the form of ideas."

According to the writer of the book, *Light-Bearers of Darkness*, which I have utilized for what I have written in the last paragraph, in the first number of Steiner's magazine, *Anthroposophy*, there was an article on Eurhythmy. Eurhythmy, it said, has grown out of the essence of Anthroposophical Spiritual Science, and is based on an understanding of the true nature of man and of his relation to the earth, as well as to the Planetary and Zodiacal Mysteries of the Cosmos. Steiner's Eurhythmy appears very suspicious.

Here as elsewhere in the literature of secret societies (René Guénon in *Le Théosophisme* treats of the exoteric and esoteric sections of the Anthroposophical Society), we find the lying statement of Satan that there is a knowledge of a life higher than that revealed and bestowed by Our Lord Jesus Christ, True God and True Man. This knowledge and this life, he suggests, are to be attained by the development of men's natural powers, and by them "they will be as gods." It is the old temptation.

But how does all this concern the making of compost for the restoration of soil-fertility? We shall see. In the book, *Compost for Garden Plot or Thousand-Acre Farm*, by Mr. F. H. Billington, formerly Inspector under the Irish Department of Agriculture, a very good summary is given of the different methods of making compost:

(a) The Bio-dynamic system based on the ideas of Dr. Rudolph Steiner

(b) The Indore method evolved by Sir Albert Howard;

(c) The Quick-Return system devised by Miss M. Bruce;

(d) The Adco method elaborated at the Rothamsted Experimental Station, England.

In Mr. Billington's summary of the Bio-dynamic method, we read such sentences as the following: "The essence of the Bio-dynamic methods lies in the conscious realization and application of fundamental life-force processes . . .. It is postulated that the earth itself is a living organism, subject to terrestrial and cosmic influences and rhythms—not a mere inert mass of matter." My readers will readily recognize the kinship between these expressions and the theories outlined above.

It is always a pleasure to come into contact with a sound outlook on life in any of its departments. Sir Albert Howard's works are amongst the most remarkable in this respect. With regard to the life of the soil, he writes: " How does humus act? Its chief function is to feed the unseen life of the soil (chiefly moulds and microbes) and also the burrowing animals like earthworms, so important in soil aeration. The wastes of this soil population, including the worms, then feed the plant. They also maintain the tilth or texture of the soil . . .. But it is not sufficient just to feed the soil population and to maintain the tilth. The soil needs a reserve of additional humus to absorb and retain water and to keep the ground warm." This quotation is taken from the chapter by Sir Albert on compost, in Mr. King's book. *There is a population living in the soil, but the soil itself is not a living organism.* In the preface to his book, *An Agricultural Testament* (Oxford University Press), Sir Albert writes as follows about the Bio-dynamic system in general: "I remain unconvinced that the disciples of Rudolph Steiner can offer any real explanation of natural laws or have yet provided any practical examples of their theories."

APPENDIX III
DESTRUCTION OF QUININE TO KEEP UP PRICE

In Chapter Five we have seen something about the systematic destruction of the gifts bestowed by God on men for their use and benefit. A particularly sad example of such destruction of portion of a valuable crop, in order to maintain a high price for the product, is given in the book entitled *Germany's Master Plan,* by Joseph Borkin and Charles. A. Welsh.[5] On pages 82 and 83 of that work we read: "It is estimated that there are some 800,000,000 sufferers from malaria in the world today, more than 100,000,000 of whom are in India alone, accounting for 1,000,000 of the 3,000,000 deaths annually. In the United States it was estimated in 1937 that there were more than 4,000,000 cases, the majority of which were in the Southern states."

"Since 1865, the Dutch have maintained one of the tightest of all monopolies by the usual methods of market control, but with consequences more immediately and dramatically tangible in the casualty lists of those stricken by malaria . . ... The 37,500 acres of [cinchona] trees [of the Dutch Quinine Syndicate's plantation in Java] supplied over 95% of the world's quinine . . ... The government sponsored syndicate of planters and manufacturers, the Kina Bureau of Amsterdam, maintained a high-price, low-output policy. Regardless of actual need or effective demand, only a limited amount of quinine was sold to each country. The annual harvests of cinchona bark... were often larger than the quotas. In such cases the excess bark was stored, or, more often, burned. It has been estimated that about 50% of the bark produced was burned in some years.

"The little quinine produced outside the Netherlands Indies was, through international agreement, subject to the same price fixing arrangements. Since the unconscionable high price occurs most frequently, the cartel's monopoly was criticized by social and medical workers in the East. The Health Section of the League of Nations . . . periodically published the production and price record of quinine and its derivatives, which so clearly bespoke the unrelenting control which had, with more efficient methods, made greater output possible, but increased prices and withheld 'surplus.' It is not too much to say that these practices were directly to blame for the continuance of a much higher death rate than that

---

[5] This book is published by John Long, Ltd., London, New York, Melbourne. The authors are officials of the United States government, but it is remarked in the Introduction by Thurman W. Arnold that their findings "have not been checked or approved in any official way."

which would have been obtained if maximum production and competitive price levels existed."

APPENDIX IV
OUTLINE OF ENGLISH HISTORY

The following brief outline of English history from Henry VIII to William of Orange, taking account of the financial factor, may prove useful to students. For the development of the points here touched upon, *The Two Nations*, by Christopher Hollis, frequently referred to in the course of this book, and *The Tragedy of the Stuarts*, by J. Desmond Gleeson (London, Cecil Palmer), are strongly recommended.

When Henry VIII attacked the Divine Plan for order, he prepared the downfall of the English popular monarchy. The families that rose to wealth and power by the confiscation of the property of the Church and the Abbey lands, which were used for the maintenance of the poor and the education of the people, gradually hemmed in the monarchy. The overthrow of the monarchy by these new fortunes of the Cecils, the Cavendishes, the Cromwells and the rest was largely contributed to by the decline in the value of money during the 16th and 17th centuries. Deriving from feudal times and customs, the normal Crown dues were fixed. While prices were rising and expenses increasing, the royal income remained at the old fixed rate. "Half an ounce of gold in Henry VIII's reign could scarcely be equaled by three ounces of gold in Charles I's reign, roughly one century later. and yet, both Henry and Charles were in receipt of incomes represented by the same figure . . .. The true royal incomes, then, were in steady decline at the same time that the private incomes of a special group of men within the state were in a condition of steady increase, And moreover, with its decreasing means, the royal resources in lands were being rapidly lost to the Crown and gained by the new men . . . . The Crown had to be subsidized and the subsidy, naturally, came from the new rich lords . . . . It was on this very question of subsidy that William Cecil and his partners were able to exercise control over Queen Elizabeth. It was in order to secure her money that she was forced to yield to their requests, notably in the matter of the public execution of Mary Queen of Scots."[6]

James I was shrewd enough to size up the situation of the monarchy and allowed Robert Cecil to guide him. Charles I "saw the dependence of the monarch upon the large owners become daily more abject, and he

---

[6] *The Tragedy of the Stuarts*, pp. 85, 86. Christopher Hollis notes that in one year at the time of the Irish campaigns Elizabeth had to sell £120,000 worth of Crown lands.

struck."[7]. By James the First's death, the price level was up to 550 and it was impossible for Charles I to pay off a debt of 5 1/2d when he had only 1d.[8] Charles I "rebelled against those who would appoint themselves his paymasters . . .. He challenged the practical rights of the new big fortunes to dictate to him because he had lost his fortune, and he lost the battle that ensued. Charles II was brought back to England from foreign exile as a salaried head of the state, almost as a salaried servant of the rich."[9] Charles, a very clever man, tried to shake himself free from the shackles with which he was bound. His experiment of issuing paper money failed, in part because, as Christopher Hollis points out, he issued his paper orders only for large sums. The bankers or goldsmiths were thus enabled to charge a large discount to those who wanted small sums and in this way brought discredit on the King's notes.[10] But the King's rising income from customs duties made him almost independent by the end of his reign.

When James II, the creator of the English fleet, who was a convinced Catholic and a man not given to compromise like Charles II, came to the throne, the wealthy nobles had a twofold reason for plotting to get rid of him. They knew that he would not be a pliable servant and they feared a Catholic reaction, which might reopen the question of the old Church lands. With the advent of William of Orange, the triumph of the aristocracy over the monarchy was complete. The foundation of the Bank of England, however, with its privilege of creating money, meant that wealth and power gradually passed into the hands of the financiers and the speculators with disastrous results for the landowners and the countryside.[11] The rule of the financiers and the speculators is called democracy.[12]

To illustrate the significance of the remark that the manipulators of money rule, in spite of the label 'democracy,' a few sentences may be quoted from an excellent pamphlet, *Money and National Reconstruction*, by P. C. Loftus, M. P. (Economic Reform Club), "That the Bank of England was

---

[7] *The Tragedy of the Stuarts*, p. 87.

[8] Cf. *The Two Nations*, p. 13.

[9] *The Tragedy of the Stuarts*, p. 87

[10] Cf. *The Two Nations*, p. 22.

[11] In the introduction to *An Agricultural Testament* (Oxford University Press), Sir Albert Howard ends his outline of the decay of the Roman Empire with the words:

"The strongest possible support of capital must always be a prosperous and contented countryside. A working compromise between agriculture and finance should, therefore, have been evolved. Failure to achieve this naturally ended in the ruin of both."

[12] Cf. the note on democracy on pp. 99–100 of *The Rulers of Russia*.

responsible for our disastrous post-war financial policy from 1920 to 1931," he writes, "is widely and, I think, correctly believed. The cardinal error of that policy was the decision to return to the gold standard, especially to return to the pre-war parity, thereby doubling the value of the depreciated pound and doubling also the real value and actual burden of our vast national debt. Warning voices were raised by individuals prominent in industry and finance pointing out that such a step must inevitably wreck the export trades and lead to a vast increase in unemployment, but in vain, and the Bank of England commenced its policy of reducing the amount of money in order to force up its value . . .. The sacrifices the nation made to restore the gold standard, the bitter years of deflation, the millions of unemployed, the ruin of the cotton and coal export were all in vain, and the edifice so laboriously constructed at such a cost of human suffering finally collapsed in 1931 . . ..Any individual may call at Somerset House and.. . inspect the shareholders' register of any public company . . .. But he is not allowed to inspect the list of shareholders of the Bank of England, if indeed a list is kept at Somerset House. Moreover, a member of Parliament is entitled to put down questions on the Order Paper of the House of Commons on almost every conceivable subject, but he is not allowed to put down any questions asking for information as to the names of the shareholders of the Bank of England."